Chambers

BOOK OF FOOTBALL FACTS

Swayam Ganguly was born and brought up in Jamshedpur, and he currently resides in Kolkata. He wears many hats, including that of a published author, director of corporate films and editorial consultant for various publishers.

Cinema and sports are his fields of passion. The early years in Jamshedpur initiated him into sports, and having played gully cricket and corporate football, he has an affinity for both the games.

Chambers BOOK OF FOOTBALL FACTS

SWAYAM GANGULY

hachette INDIA

First published in 2024 by Hachette India
(Registered name: Hachette Book Publishing India Pvt. Ltd)
An Hachette UK company
www.hachetteindia.com

Chambers® is a registered trademark of Chambers Harrap Publishers Ltd, an Hachette UK company

1

ISBN 978-93-5731-981-2

Hachette Book Publishing India Pvt. Ltd
4th & 5th Floors, Corporate Centre,
Plot No. 94, Sector 44, Gurugram 122003, India

Typeset in Sabon 11/14.2
by InoSoft Systems, Noida

Printed and bound in India
by Manipal Technologies Limited

FSC
www.fsc.org
MIX
Paper | Supporting responsible forestry
FSC™ C043100

CONTENTS

PREFACE

Welcome to the world's greatest game!

Football isn't just played; it is lived. From the first kick-off to the final whistle, it's a riveting 90-minute drama that unfolds on pitches from the streets of Brazil through the floodlit arenas of Europe to the streets of Kolkata. And this book is your ultimate guide to understanding and loving every moment of it.

Chambers Book of Football Facts is not just a book – it's everything football; a deep dive, more than just a match on a pitch. It's pre-match prep too – the rules of the game, from the offside trap to the VAR debates.

Journey through top leagues and tournaments that make the football world go round – from the Champions League that produces legends to the intense battles of La Liga and the Premier League. Along the way, discover the origins of football and how it evolved into the high-octane spectacle it is today. And of course the legends of the game, those players whose names are etched in football history – the wizards with the magic feet, the maestros who see two steps ahead, and the heroes who've turned matches around with a single touch. From Maradona's Goal of the Century to Cristiano Ronaldo's epic freekicks, from the Cruyff Turn to Messidependencia, know the moments that made stars into the GOATs.

This book isn't just for those who know the difference between a 4–4–2 and a 3–5–2. Whether one is lacing up for the first time or has been kicking the ball around for years – this book offers something for everyone. Beyond the touchline, this book dives into the vibrant culture that makes football more than just a game. Readers will explore iconic stadiums that are cathedrals to the faithful, the chants that echo through the ages, and the technology that is shaping the future of the sport. It also touches on the strange, the bizarre, and the downright unbelievable – because in football, all is possible. It's more than just facts and figures; it's a love letter to the game that unites us all, a tribute to the artistry, drama, and pure joy that only football delivers.

And this book goes to extra time. With QR codes linking to videos of iconic goals, saves, and unforgettable moments, one can relive the magic as if they were right there in the stands. Whether it's the Dutch team's Total Football, crazy goal celebrations, or Beckham's corner kick, these moments aren't just history – they're living, breathing pieces of football's soul. Relive the magic anytime, anywhere.

So lace up your boots, step onto the pitch, and feel the adrenaline. From the first whistle to the final kick, the world of football is waiting for you – and with this book in hand, you're ready to take it on.

1

THE SEVENTEEN LAWS OF FOOTBALL

IT IS A KNOWN FACT THAT FOOTBALL IS A TEAM SPORT THAT is played with two teams of eleven players each competing on a football field to outplay and outscore each other. But what most people do not know is that both the teams have to adhere to a set of as many as seventeen regulations, which are enforced and maintained in a particular game of football by the referee and the other officials. The following are the seventeen football rules that govern this beautiful game.

'The Laws of the Game' were first codified in 1863 when the Football Association (FA) was established in England, where modern football was invented. The laws have changed over time since then and have been maintained by the International Football Association Board (IFAB) since 1866.

Law 1: THE FIELD OF PLAY

The first law of football determines the size and the markings of the football field, also known as a football pitch or field. Natural or artificial grass is used to make the surface of this football field. Amateur football matches also take place in dirt grounds.

The football ground or pitch is rectangular in shape and is divided into two equal halves by a line running parallel to the goal line, and this marks the playing surface. This line also serves as the centre of the pitch with a circle measuring 9.15 m drawn around it. The longer sides are called touchlines and the shorter sides, goal lines. The two goal lines are of the same length and are between 45 and 90 m wide. The two touchlines, also of the same length, are between 90 and 120 m long. All lines on the football ground are equally wide, and the corners of the ground are marked by corner flags because it is from here that corner kicks are taken towards the goal post.

For international football matches, the dimensions of the football field are more tightly constrained as the goal lines are between 64 and 75 m wide and the touchlines are between 110 and 110 m long.

The centre circle is marked at 9.15 m from the centre mark. This is similar to the penalty arc in front of the goal and indicates the minimum distance that players from the opposing team have to be from each other at kick-off. The ball is placed right in the centre at kick-off and again when a goal is scored.

The pitch is divided in two by the halfway line, with the half in which a football team is playing known as their half. The arcs in the corners denote the area in which the ball has to be placed for corner kicks, and this is within one yard of the corner denoted by the corner flag. During a corner, opposition players have to be 9.15 m away from the ball.

The term goal line refers to the complete line at either end of the pitch from one corner flag to the other and not just the line between the goalposts.

The goalposts, which are guarded by goalkeepers, are placed at the centre of each goal line. Goalposts comprise two upright posts placed equidistant from the corner flag posts, and the two posts are joined by a horizontal pole at the top, which is known as the crossbar. The inner edges of the posts have to be 7.32 m or 24 feet wide or apart, and the lower edge of the crossbar is elevated to 2.44 m or 8 feet above the pitch. Nets are placed behind the goal, and surprisingly, this netting, which has become so integral to the modern game and commentary, is not required or mentioned by the laws. The laws further state that goalposts and crossbars have to be white and made either of wood, metal or other approved material. However, to safeguard against goalpost collisions and injuries, a variety of materials are used in the modern game to coat goalposts. An example of such a desirable mixture would be one made of 63 per cent the weight of methyl methacrylate, 32 per cent by the weight of polyethylene glycol, and cross linked with 5 per cent the weight of ethylene glycol dimethacrylate. This is perfect for player safety and preservation of damage to the goalpost under player impact.

A goal is scored in football when the ball fully crosses the goal line between the goalposts and beneath the crossbar, even if a defending player touched the ball before it did so. When this happens, it is termed as an own goal. A goal may be considered illegal and declared null and void by the officiating referee if the player scoring a goal or any of his team members commit an offence under the laws of the game, like a foul being committed. The goal may also be ruled out because of an offside when the member of a team is in an offside position. Being offside is when there are no defenders between the goalkeeper and the attacker.

In a football field, grass is the normal surface of play, although artificial turf is used sometimes, especially in areas where grass does not grow because of heavy snowfall, like the colder Nordic countries and countries where grass cannot be maintained properly due to inclement weather.

Amazing Facts about the Field of Play

- Professional pitches can vary in size significantly across the globe. Most Premier League football pitches in England measure 115 yards (105.16 m) x 74 yards (67.67 m). However, Wembley Stadium's pitch dimensions are 115 yards (105.16 m) long by 75 yards (68.58 m) wide.
- FIFA and FA regulations state that the dimensions of an eleven-a-side football pitch must be between 100 and 130 yards (90–120 m) long, and 50 and 100 yards (45–90 m) wide.
- The International Space Station (ISS) and a football field are almost the same size. The International Space Station measures 357 feet end to end. That's almost equivalent to the length of a football field, including the end zones (360 feet). The scientist who designed the ISS must have been an avid football fan!

Football Field

- Stadium 974 in Qatar was the first-ever temporary football stadium used in a World Cup game. It was constructed using shipping containers and dismantled after the game.
- Greenland can never host any official football games despite having a decent football team. This is because the weather in Greenland is just too cold for grass to grow, which is an essential requirement from FIFA to host an official game. Go green, Greenland!

The Seven Wonders of Football Pitches

Here's a list of the seven most scenic football pitches in the world. So what if Greenland is not so green for football. These seven wonders of football certainly are and then some. Even if you aren't a football fan, they are worthy of a visit.

1. The Ottmar Hitzfeld Stadium in Zermatt, Switzerland is a football pitch that is 2,000 m above sea level. Located in the Swiss Alps, this is perfect for a game of five-a-side football. High-altitude training is highly recommended before you kick the ball though.
2. Can you imagine that there's a football pitch that actually floats on water? The Floating Pitch is located at Phang Nga, Thailand. If you want to play football here, you need to be a good swimmer as well in case you kick the ball right into the water and have to retrieve it. So, keep your swimming trunks handy along with your football gear.
3. The amazing Adidas Futsal Park in Tokyo, Japan, is located on a fully enclosed high-rise high in the Tokyo sky much above the hustle and bustle of the capital city below. Thankfully, there's no chance of losing the ball on this pitch.
4. The Float at Marina Bay, Singapore, is a pitch that's rocking and fast. No wonder this multifunctional floating platform is used for rock concerts, the Formula 1 race, and as a football pitch. With a capacity of 27,000 spectators, it is just right for playing football at night under floodlights.
5. Iceland is one of the most scenic countries in the world, and naturally, their football pitches are seriously scenic. But the top honour goes to Hásteinsvöllur, which is a club ground nestled among jutting cliff faces.

You might want to combine hiking with football to get the best of both worlds.

6. If you are a football fanatic visiting Ireland, you might want to tick the remote and beautiful Inishturk Island on your bucket list. It's located off the Irish west coast, and although technically a pitch for Gaelic football or hurling, it also serves as a football field. Chances are you might want to stop playing and admire the stunning views on offer.
7. The Henningsvær Stadium in Lofoten, Norway, is a dream football pitch. Probably the most scenic of all places where you can play football, you have to first pass through a small Norwegian village to reach this ground.

Henningsvær Stadium, Lofoten, Norway

Law 2: THE BALL

The second law of football lays the specifications about the size, shape and material composition of the ball or the football. The law specifies that the ball is an air-filled sphere and that the standard diameter of a size 5 ball must be about 22 cm with a circumference of 68–70 cm and a weight between 410 and 450 kg. The ball must be inflated to a pressure of 0.6 to 1.1 atmospheres at 'sea level' and has to be covered in leather or any other suitable material.

Natural materials were used to make the first balls, like inflated pig bladder, which was placed inside a leather cover. However, modern footballs are designed by a team of engineers with rubber or plastic bladders, often with plastic covers, and great precision is employed to reach the exact specifications and create the finest football.

The weight of the ball has been clearly specified today as problems arose when the older balls became considerably heavier during the matches played in wet conditions. Today, modern Association footballs are created by stitching together as many as 32 panels of waterproofed leather or plastic so that the ball remains the same irrespective of match conditions or inclement weather. The 32-panel configuration is a spherical polyhedron made up of 12 regular pentagons and 20 regular hexagons. All this for a football, you might say. Well, it's the most popular sport in the world after all, with nearly all the countries in the world playing the sport. So, the ball has to be special.

The first 32-panel ball was marketed by Select in Denmark in the 1950s. This configuration of the football gained in popularity and was accepted by all of Continental Europe in the 1960s. Adidas Telstar propagated this ball worldwide, and it became the official ball of the 1970 World Cup.

However, mass production of footballs began in 1888 as a direct consequence of the founding of the English Football League in the same year. To meet the growing demands for footballs, Mitre and Thomlinson's of Glasgow became two of the first companies to mass-produce footballs then. The key element in a quality football was thought to be how well it could retain its shape. The strength of the leather and the skills of the cutters and stitchers were the main factors to produce the desired football. The top-grade covers were made with leather from the rump of a cow, while the lower-quality footballs were made from the shoulder. Advances in ball design arrived later as the interlocking panels were developed instead of the previously used leather sections that met at the north and south poles of the ball. The footballs were then produced with a more acceptable round shape.

Fantastic Fun Facts About the Football

- Footballs have been around much longer than you or I. In fact, the ball has been there for centuries. A game resembling football was played more than 2,000 years ago in China, Rome, and Greece. It's certainly the oldest ball game played by man.
- The oldest football in existence is more than 430 years old and was discovered during an excavation at Stirling Castle in Scotland in the 1970s. This

football, made of leather (probably from a deer) and pig's bladder, is estimated to have been made circa 1550 and was discovered on the roof of Stirling Castle. What it was doing there all these years is anyone's guess. It weighs 125 g and is currently on display at the Stirling Smith Art Gallery and Museum.

- The football had four variations in its early history. The Chinese version of the ball had stuffed animal skin rolled into a ball. The Egyptians used linen pouches filled with different seeds to play ball. The Aztecs and Mayans preferred balls made from latex harvested from rubber trees. The Greeks followed the Egyptian practice but replaced the seeds in linen pouches with hair.
- It was not always that ancient footballs were made using plants or animal parts. The Mesoamerican culture preferred kicking around severed heads during a game. They did so to honour a myth that stated if a man loses a game in the underworld, he has to lose his head. This myth caused serious problems as players who lost a game had to lose their heads as well. They certainly never ran out of balls to play with!
- If you run out of heads to play with, use skulls instead. That's what a pre-medieval legend seems to suggest. An entire village would kick a skull along the path to a nearby village square before the invention of the football. The opponents in the other village would attempt to kick this skull back to the square of the

first village. That's how the first riots began in football games presumably.

- Charles Goodyear had a relatively good year in 1855 when he invented the rubber vulcanization process. What's even better is that he decided to fashion a football out of his invention and revolutionized football. It was a good move as it created a rubber ball that did not become deformed or melt because of exposure to high temperatures. Good on you, Charles!
- In 1862, H.J. Lindon developed a kind of inflatable rubber that made a better football. Lindon's wife had passed away before this from lung disease, caused reportedly from blowing up hundreds of pig's bladders. This probably inspired the deceased's husband to fashion the inflatable rubber bladder. Now, the ball could retain its shape longer, remaining nice, hard, and oval, and it was easier to play with and hit the target more accurately.
- The standard football we know was not always black and white, and this familiar pattern only came about during the 1970 World Cup. Adidas created this design called the Telstar.
- The 32 panels in a football were designed keeping the 32 European nations in mind. The rest of the world, especially Latin America, might have something to say about that. They must have actually, as the ball designed for the 2006 World Cup had just 14 panels. Then, the 2010 World Cup had a ball with eight panels and a six-panel football was kicked around during the 2014 World Cup. Soon, panels

will be out of existence at the rate at which we are going.

- The football was kicked the fastest in 2001 at the studios of El Show de los Récords, Madrid, Spain, when Spain's Francisco Javier Galan Màrin kicked it much harder than those medieval villagers ever kicked their skull. This was the record for the fastest kick in football when Marin made the ball travel at 129 km/hour. That's faster than the full speed of a cheetah, which is the fastest land animal. But despite the heroics, Spain has won the World Cup only once to date. Speed's not everything after all!

Law 3: THE PLAYERS

Law 3 states that eleven players should be playing on the field in each team. Out of the playing eleven, one must be the goalkeeper, and the players must hit the ball with either their legs or torso. Other than the goalkeeper, no one is allowed to use their hands or arms to touch the ball, and the goalkeeper is allowed to use his hands only in the penalty box and not outside the box. A team must have at least seven players to be considered complete and play a football match.

Unbelievable Facts about Early Goalkeepers

- Before football rules were formalized, goalkeepers could gather the ball with their hands anywhere on the football pitch and were not restricted to doing so only in the penalty box. The rules were then restricted later but only by half. Now, the goalkeeper could still gather the ball with his hands in his own half. Imagine such a scenario in today's football. There would be more 'Hand of God' goals for sure!

- Any player, not necessarily only the goalkeeper, could catch the ball during football's early days. However, they were not allowed to run with the ball or throw it into the goal. If a player caught the ball, he was awarded a free kick if he made an impression on the pitch after the fair catch. Catch me if you can!
- Goalkeepers found it difficult not to concede a goal as, for a long time, there was no standard goal size. This meant that sometimes, a goalpost stretched from one tree to another or from one door to the other. Even the most dedicated and talented goalkeepers of today wouldn't have stopped the goals back then as they kept flowing. Some games had as many as fifteen goalkeepers to save the goal, more as a punishment than an ultra-defensive measure. These were the less athletic people who were made to stand at the goal as punishment for their lack of physical stamina or skill. Even the great LM10 or CR7 couldn't get the ball past fifteen goalkeepers surely.
- Goalkeepers did not have a dedicated presence in the playing teams as long as all of them could handle the ball in the field of play. The player closest to the goalpost usually doubled up as the goalkeeper. This alarming trend changed, thankfully, in the 1860s when it was a must for dedicated goalkeepers to be a part of the playing eleven. 1909 saw the introduction of a

different coloured jersey for goalkeepers to distinguish them from the other players on their team.

- The early goalkeepers also did not wear gloves back then. The first goalkeeper to do so was Argentinean goalie Amadeo Carrizo playing for River Plate in the 1940s and '50s. The trend in gloves started when some goalkeepers began experimenting with household items like gardening gloves or rubber kitchen gloves to grip the ball better, especially in slippery conditions.

Law 4: THE PLAYERS' EQUIPMENT

Law 4 states that every player must wear a shirt, shorts, socks, shoes and proper shin protection as per the rules. Though it's not mandatory, footballers may wear headgear if they choose to. We saw the famous goalkeeper Petr Čech wearing headgear during his playing days. Players are not permitted to wear or use any equipment that might prove harmful to them or other players, like rings, for example. The goalkeeper has to be dressed differently than the other players on the pitch, as well as the match officials like the referees and the linesmen.

Amazing Facts about Football Shoes or Cleats

- The first known documented pair of football shoes or cleats was created by an English royal shoemaker named Cornelius Johnson for King Henry VIII. However, the first studded sandals that inspired football boots are thought to have been issued first to the Roman legionaries.

- Cleats provide traction for footballers on the pitch. It makes it easier for them to grip the ground and change direction quickly to avoid injuries.
- Before proper cleats were invented, footballers used to play in their work boots by fashioning cleats out of them with a steel toecap. Studs or tacks were hammered to the bottom of the boot to gain more traction in the playing area. But these boots were not only heavy but dangerous to the other players.
- In 1863, after the development of the FA, the safety of the players became paramount, and priority was given to a safer and more functional football shoe. The heavier ankle boots were replaced by lighter boots made of vulcanized rubber and six rounded studs.
- The iconic invention of replaceable studs on football shoes was made by the famous German brothers Adolf and Rudolf. They opened the Dassler Brothers Shoe Factory, which made these studs that could be changed as per the playing conditions on the field. But the brothers soon parted ways to create two famous shoe brands we know today as Puma and Adidas.
- Football boots remained a constant for a long time, and further modifications were made only after World War II. The new cleats were lighter and more flexible. They also featured lower cut tops that allowed free ankle movement on the football pitch.
- New materials and colours were added to the cleats in the 1970s. In 1979, Adidas used kangaroo leather and a great design to create the famous Copa Mundial cleats.

Football Cleats

- The '80s saw a new style introduced by Adidas when Craig Johnston created the Predator by using polymer extrusion technology that increased flexibility in the soles of the boots. The rounded studs were replaced with a bladed design for more traction on the field. The Predator boots became very popular.
- The '90s saw several brands competing with each other to create the best football cleats, with Puma, Adidas and Nike among the top three. The top brands started paying popular footballers to wear their unique designs during football matches, thus giving birth to celebrity endorsements.
- Adidas and Nike are the two biggest football cleat manufacturers in the world today. We are sure to see more improved designs from them in the near future.

Law 5: THE REFEREE

The official who oversees a football game or is in charge of its affairs is called a referee. The referee has the last say in all matters on the football pitch, and in recent times, technology has helped the cause of the referee. The referee is armed with a whistle and two cards called yellow and red cards. 2 yellows and 1 red card have a player sent off the football pitch. The referee is ably assisted by two linesmen, known as assistant referees today.

Funniest Referee Moments

- English Premier League (EPL) Birmingham City footballer Robbie Savage was a naughty boy on the pitch who loved playing pranks. But even Robbie wasn't ready for the savage treatment meted out to him by a referee. Birmingham City were playing Newcastle United when referee Matt Messias accidentally whacked the Welsh midfielder in the face, giving Savage a bloody nose. This immediately prompted Newcastle striker Alan Shearer to jokingly give the referee a red card!
- Just like a footballer, the ultimate dream of a referee is to participate in a World Cup by officiating in it. In 2006, English referee Graham Poll realized this dream, and the fact that he was England's only official in the tournament also made it a special achievement. But things went horribly wrong for Poll in a group game match between Croatia and Australia. He erroneously gave Croatian defender Josip Šimunić as many as 3

yellow cards before sending him off the field, whereas Šimunić should have exited the field after receiving 2 yellow cards. Graham Poll's World Cup dream ended as he was sent home shortly after this match.

- Cut to the present in 2024, when a bizarre incident saw a 61-year-old Dutch referee banned for life for celebrating the title success with the winning team. Referee Jan Smit from Opmeer in North Netherlands officiated in the title match between fourth division teams St. George and SV De Valken. St. George scored the winning goal in stoppage time, but the referee helped them with 15 minutes of time added on and sending off three players of SV De Valken, who finished the match with eight players. To add insult to injury, the referee also celebrated St. George's title win. Smit got on the podium, sang songs, and lifted the trophy. Following a complaint from De Valken, the Dutch football federation suspended Smit for life. Bizarre!
- Sometimes, referees get frustrated too, with all the pressure and expectations. But surely that's no excuse to kick a player. French referee Tony Chapron certainly doesn't think so. During the 2017–18 season of the French League, Chapron was officiating in a match between Nantes and Paris Saint-Germain (PSG) when he suddenly lost his cool. He kicked out at Nantes footballer Diego Carlos after a clash in the centre of the field of play. If that wasn't enough, the referee also red-carded Diego Carlos for the incident. The referee was banned from football for six months.

Pierluigi Collina during the UEFA Euro 2004

- Just when you thought French referees were funny, another English referee will make you feel he is the contender to the throne of the funniest referee in football. Stuart Attwell was officiating in a 2008 match between Reading and Watford when a Reading header went wide. To the delight of the Reading players, Attwell awarded a goal. However, everyone was stunned at this strange decision, except Attwell, of course. It was arguably the worst decision in football.
- Legendary referee Pierluigi Collina was as famous for his icy-cold stares and bald look as his physical

fitness, his refereeing decisions, as well as his ability to control a difficult game. Regarded as one of the best referees in football history, Collina never let a star footballer intimidate him. He absolutely bossed the game, never addressing the players by their names but by their jersey numbers. Famous phrases include, 'Number 10, shut up!' or 'Number 4, come here!' It also helped that Collina was 6 feet 2 inches and few players could tower over him. There'll never be another like Collina.

- Then, there's the curious case of the drunk referee from Belarus. Sergey Shmolik had the distinction of officiating in an England versus Luxembourg game in 1999. But what shot him into the high league of referees was his performance in a Belarus league game during which he was on a liquid diet. Poor Sergey was so sloshed that he stood in the centre of the pitch and barely moved. Another official had to carry him off from the pitch after the game. No surprise that he was suspended by the Belarus FA after the game.
- We've saved the funniest for the last, and it's no surprise that the incident took place in South America, where the sport is literally a different ball game. In a shocking incident at the Starling Soares Stadium in south-east Brazil, referee Camilo Eustáquio de Souza pulled a gun on a player after getting punched in the face and receiving a black eye. After the referee had awarded a penalty, amateur player Marcos Lopes Vieira angrily confronted him, and after a heated exchange, displayed his boxing skills. Big mistake!

The part-time referee, who was a cop in real life, ran to the bench to take out his gun and handcuffs from his bag. When Vieira saw the referee running back holding something that didn't resemble a red card, he ran for his life to jump the stadium fence and sought sanctuary in the dressing room. The referee insisted later that all he was trying to do was take the player into custody. Never a dull moment in Brazilian football as they say!

Law 6: THE OTHER MATCH OFFICIALS

The referee is ably assisted by the two assistant referees or linesmen who help maintain the decorum of the game. They are placed on either side of the football field and help the referee gauge offside positions, offences, and if or not the ball has crossed the line.

Linesmen were introduced to football in 1891, primarily to ascertain if the ball was in or out of play as well as to indicate throw-ins, goal kicks and corner kicks. But over the years, the role of the linesman transformed drastically. The biggest transformation took place in 1996 when they were given the responsibility of indicating if a player was in an offside position or had committed an offence and to communicate the same to the referee. 1996 also saw the renaming of linesmen and lineswomen to assistant referee/s on account of the broader job responsibilities assigned to them. The reason for the change of the term was also because of the need for gender neutrality. However, the term linesman (or linesmen) is still in use in many footballing countries.

Bizarre On-the-line and Off-the-line Moments

- One of the funniest moments in a football match involving an assistant referee was in a Ghanaian Premier League match. The African linesman was so engrossed in the game between Asante Kotoko and Bibiani Gold Stars that he left his position on the line. As Asante Kotoko mounted a threatening attack, the assistant referee abandoned his position and encroached into the field of play, almost joining in. He had almost entered the 18-yard area by the time the ball hit the crossbar and went in. In his exuberance, the linesman completely forgot his call of duty and the fact that he wasn't in the playing eleven.
- During a Russian Premier League game between reserve teams, Russian linesman Musa Kadyrov decided to take matters into his own hands when he was abused by a young defender. The match was between Terek Grozny and Amkar Perm in the city of Grozny in the Chechnya region. Eighteen-year-old Amkar Perm defender Ilya Krichmar abused the linesman. In retaliation Kadyrov punched Krichmar and kicked him as he lay on the ground. Cases of referees and assistant referees assaulting players are extremely rare as the opposite often holds true.
- In a 2014–15 match, Atletico Madrid found themselves exiting the Copa del Rey against Barcelona. Atletico Madrid player Arda Turan was so angry with the apparent error of the linesman that he threw his boot at the assistant referee. Strangely, Turan received just a yellow card for the offence instead of a red.

Law 7: THE DURATION OF THE MATCH

Law 7 states that the duration of a football match is 90 minutes long, which is divided into two halves of 45 minutes each. Between the two halves, there is a half-time break of 15 minutes. The full time of 90 minutes marks the conclusion of the game. However, a knockout game has two periods of extra time of 15 minutes each if the two teams are still locked goalless after 90 minutes. Even if that fails to provide a result, the match is then decided in a penalty shoot-out where each team takes five penalty shots. The one scoring the most goals wins. If they still tie, then sudden death takes place.

The Longest Professional Football Match in Recorded History

- The face-off between English clubs Stockport County and Doncaster Rovers that took place on 30 March 1946 at Edgeley Park is the longest football match in recorded history. The match went on for an astonishing three hours and 23 minutes, and this world record has stood for more than half a century. This was before the invention of penalty shoot-outs, and the match ended 2–2 after 90 minutes. The 30 minutes of extra time did not produce any goals, and the 'play to win' rule came into effect, which was a form of golden goal. Whoever scored first would win. Stockport found the net in the 173rd minute, but the goal was disallowed by the referee. So, the two sides played on and on till it became too dark to play as floodlights hadn't been invented. Surprisingly, this drawn match was a replay as the earlier match had also been drawn 2–2. A coin toss decided the hosts of the second replay. Doncaster Rovers won the toss and the next match on their home ground, demolishing Stockport County 4–0.

Law 8: THE START AND RESTART OF PLAY

Every football game begins with a toss as the two captains meet in the middle of the pitch with the match referee. After the toss decides which team plays in which half, the team losing the toss kicks off the game. After half-time or 45 minutes of play, the teams interchange positions in the halves of the field.

The Strangest Kick-Off?

- Scotland's World Cup qualifier in Estonia in 1996 has got to be one of the strangest kick-offs in the history of football if not the strangest. Because of inadequate floodlights in the Estonian stadium, FIFA ordered that the match be brought forward by three hours. But the home side simply refused to turn up, stating insufficient notice. Scotland was left without an opposition but still did not win the match, which was a farce really. At 3 p.m. sharp, the game kicked off, and after a few passes that lasted three seconds, the referee blew his whistle to end the farce/match. FIFA ordered a replay of the match, and the Scots were held to a goalless draw by Estonia in Monaco. This must have led to jokes in England as to how the Scots couldn't win even if an opposition wasn't present. But that's a different story.

Bizarre Stoppage and Delay of Play

- A 1977 league match in England between Manchester City and Derby County had a bizarre stoppage of play. When Derby County was awarded a penalty towards the end of the match, it was noticed that there was so little grass on the pitch that it was unclear where the penalty spot actually was. So, play had to be paused for the groundsman to repaint the penalty spot. The fans, players and officials waited patiently as the groundsman made his appearance, armed with a paint bucket and tape measure to do the needful. The penalty kick was duly converted by Derby County despite the delay.

Law 9: THE BALL IN AND OUT OF PLAY

The ball in play and the ball out of play are the two primary stages of play during a football match. The ball is in play during a football match from kick-off to the end of the game except when it goes out of the field occasionally or the referee stops the game for the ball to be out of play.

Bizarre Zaire Strategy

- Zaire made their maiden appearance in the 1974 World Cup and is remembered for the wrong reason. When Zaire faced Brazil, the South American superpower had a free kick perilously close to the Zaire goal. As the Brazilians got ready to take the free kick, the strangest thing happened. Zaire player Mwepu Ilunga suddenly broke away from the defensive wall

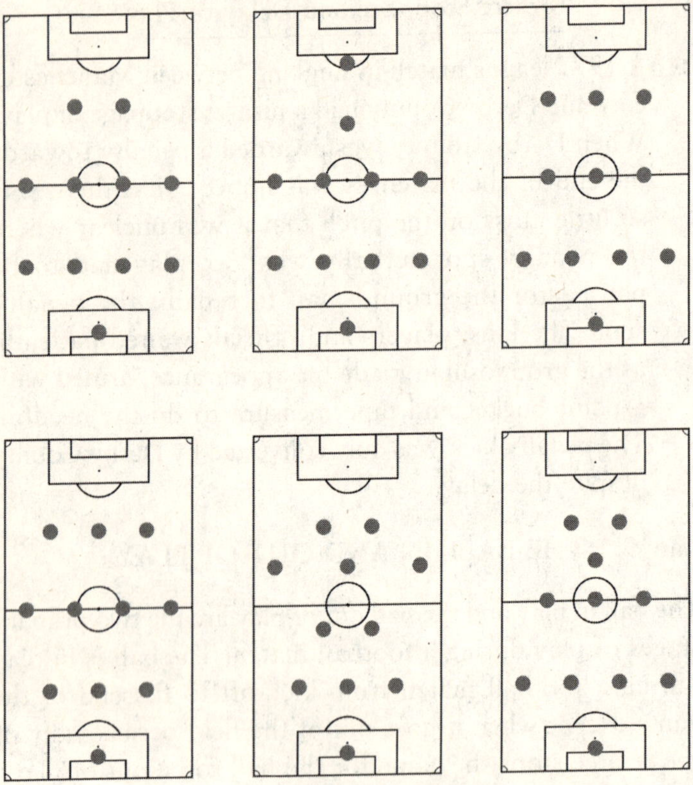

Attack Tactics in Football

and kicked the ball out of play. If this moment was weird, Ilunga's claim later was even stranger. He said he was aware of the rules and did this deliberately to distract the opponents. He was booked, and the free kick was taken again. Brazil won the match 3–0. It was revealed later that he did this to protest against the dictatorial regime in Zaire.

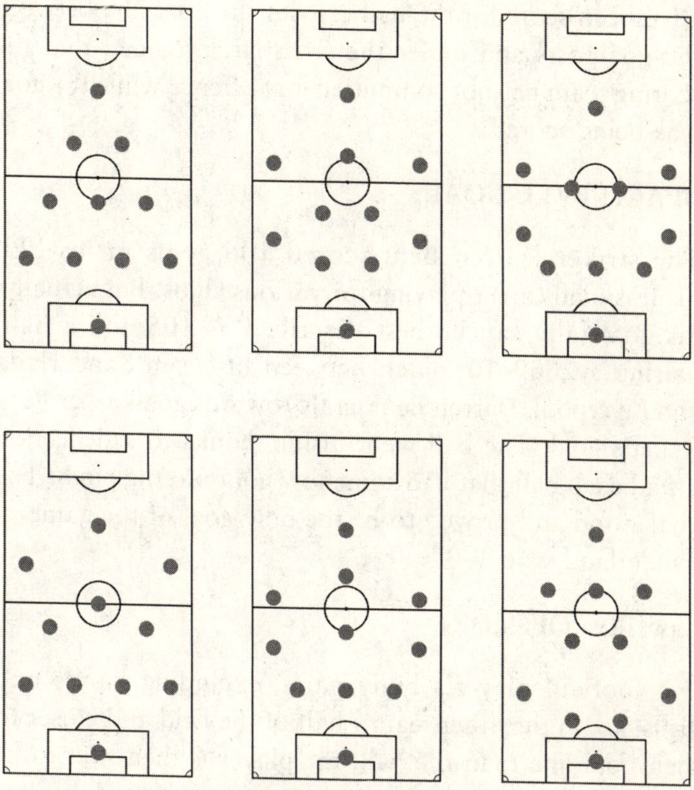

Defence Tactics in Football

Law 10: DETERMINING THE OUTCOME OF A MATCH

The objective of a football match is to score more goals than the opponent team by making the ball cross the goal line of the opponent team's goalpost. A goal is said to have been scored if the ball crosses the goal line between the goalposts and under the crossbar, provided that the scoring team has not committed any offence while the goal was being scored.

BEACH BALL GOAL

The striker Darren Bent scored 106 goals in his EPL professional career playing for various clubs. But actually, his goal tally can be best described as 105 and a half. During a 2009–10 match between his team Sunderland and Liverpool, Darren Bent let fly towards goalkeeper Pepe Reina's goal. The ball went inside thanks to a deflection off a beach ball that had somehow got onto the pitch. The goal stood and proved to be the only goal of the game as Sunderland won 1–0.

Law 11: OFFSIDE

If a football player's body parts, excluding hands and arms, are in the other team's half of the field and closer to their goal line than the ball, the player is then said to be in an offside position. There are no opposition defenders between the player and the goalkeeper of the opponent team. Being in an offside position is not an offence, but a player who is in that position uses that as an unfair advantage to their team.

What Is an Offside Trap in Football?

The offside trap in football is a technique employed by defenders of a side to stop the opposition attack before it can threaten them by resulting in a goal. This happens when all the defensive players step up the pitch just enough right before a pass is made by the opponent team to their striker. If this is done the right way, which it is most often, the only player between the opponent team's striker and the goal is the goalkeeper. The pioneer of the offside trap was Notts County, and the offside trap came into football in the 1900s. Since then, it has been a key element of every team's defensive strategy to stop an attack by the opposition.

Amazing Offside Facts

- Ever since VAR or video assistant referee was introduced in international football in 2016, a second check on offside calls that have led to goals has become possible. VAR is nothing but an extra match official seated in front of a video screen whose job is to review the referee's decisions when necessary.
- Linesmen or assistant referees often do not signal offsides when the moves have the potential to score goals. Only after the goal is scored does the linesman signal for outside to make the goal null and void. The VAR then checks the linesman's call with the aid of video footage and technology. VAR can also overturn the decision and re-award the goal if the linesman was erroneous in his decision as made clear by the video replay. VAR decisions are communicated only to the referee officiating the game.
- The great French maestro Zinedine Zidane was very rarely caught in an offside position during his entire football career. That is some serious achievement,

especially since the man scored so many spectacular goals.

- The record for the maximum offsides in the EPL belongs to Emmanuel Adebayor, with a staggering 328 offsides playing for Tottenham Hotspur. That's way too many actually. It's almost as if the man from Togo loved being in an offside position as no other reason explains this baffling record.

Law 12: FOULS AND MISCONDUCT

A foul is committed in a football match when a player goes against the laws or rules of the game and subsequently prevents the game from being played. The opposition team of the player who commits the foul is given a free kick as punishment for breaking the rule. The referee may discipline the player who has committed the foul by giving him a yellow card as a warning or sending him off the field with a red card according to the severity of the foul committed. A player who is sent off the field after receiving 2 yellow cards or 1 red card by the referee cannot be replaced in the field of play.

FIVE OF THE WORST FOULS IN FOOTBALL HISTORY

Thomas Müller

German footballer Thomas Müller's foul in the Champions League 2018 was dreadful. It was a hard-fought battle between Bayern Munich and Ajax, with both teams having scored a goal apiece. In the 76th minute, Müller tried to reach a long ball but kicked an Ajax player directly in the head with his boots. In Müller's defence, he didn't see the Ajax player, but he was sent off for this dreadful foul. Luckily, the Ajax player could continue playing after receiving treatment on the pitch.

Roy Keane

In the 1997 match between Manchester United and Leeds, Roy Keane and Alf Inge Haaland clashed many times. Just before the game ended, Keane tried to trip Haaland but got injured himself. Haaland shouted at Keane to stop faking an injury. But Keane had actually injured himself and had to sit out for a long time. The two met again in a match three and a half years later, and now, Haaland was playing for Manchester City. Keane had his mind set on revenge, and his dangerous tackle on Haaland earned Keane a red card and a 5,000-pound fine. A year later, Keane wrote in his autobiography that he just wanted to hurt Haaland with his foul. He was promptly handed another 5-match ban and a fine of 1,50,000 pounds. Sadly, his knee injury forced Haaland to retire after spending ten years of his career in the EPL. But that's not the end of the story. Alf Inge Haaland's son Erling Haaland became the superstar of the Premier League years later. But he was not too keen on joining Manchester United when they bid for him. We are guessing the reason is Roy Keane's incident with his father.

Nigel de Jong

The Netherlands faced Spain in a crucial encounter in the 2010 World Cup. In the 28th minute, when the match was still goalless, Dutchman Nigel de Jong fouled Spaniard Xavi Alonso with a kung fu kick to the chest. The Spaniards were angry when Nigel de Jong escaped with just a yellow card for that grievous offence. Thankfully, Alonso recovered to continue playing, and the Spaniards forgot their anger when they won that World Cup.

Harald Schumacher

France and Germany clashed in a high-voltage semi-final game in the 1982 World Cup. French player Battiston took a shot at the German goal as Harald Schumacher raced towards him. Battiston missed the target, but Schumacher didn't. He jumped into the air, and his hip smashed into the Frenchman's face in one of the worst fouls ever. Battiston lost several teeth and injured his spine. Surprisingly, not even a yellow card was shown by the referee to Schumacher. Germany entered the final to be beaten by Italy. That's French karma for you!

Norbert Siegmann

In 1981, in a match between Werder Bremen and Arminia Bielefeld, Ewald Lienen tried to dribble past Norbert Siegmann and was tackled heavily, causing a serious injury. Siegmann's studs slit Lienen's thigh open to cause a deep, open wound that exposed the muscles and femur bone. Lienen recovered from the injury after four weeks and sued Siegmann, as well as his coach because the players had been encouraged by their coach to foul. The lawsuit failed, but as the news spread, the coach received death threats and sat on the bench wearing a bulletproof vest in the next game.

Law 13: FREE KICKS

Free kicks awarded by the referees were categorized into two – indirect free kicks and direct free kicks. Serious offences like handballs and foul play lead to a direct free kick awarded by the referee, while indirect free kicks are given for less serious offences. In indirect free kicks, the ball must touch a player before it crosses the goal line, while a goal can be scored directly from a direct free kick.

Top Ten Free Kick Goalscorers

10. Portuguese Cristiano Ronaldo or CR7 is at Number 10 for the highest free kicks scored in football with 64 goals. He is still going strong with his classic deep breath and four-step free kick run-up, and it shouldn't be a surprise at all if he moves considerably up the ladder.
9. Rogério Ceni is next on the list with 61 goals, but what makes his achievement special is that he's a goalkeeper who also scored goals. The Brazilian lit up the pitch for Sao Paolo throughout the 1990s and 2000s, scoring 131 goals, 61 of which came from free kicks. When he was not scoring goals, Ceni was busy saving them.
8. The great Diego Maradona from Argentina is eighth on the list with 62 goals. Besides his dribbling and play-making skills, Maradona was a true free-kick specialist.
7. Zico, the great Brazilian No.10, is seventh on the list. His creative abilities and technical vision made him

Rogério Ceni

a great free-kick taker with 62 career goals from free kicks.

6. Bend it like Beckham! The result is 65 goals from free kicks in a great career with England and clubs like Manchester United and Real Madrid among others. The poster boy of English football once upon a time is sixth on the list.
5. The little Argentinean football wizard Lionel Messi has converted some delightful set pieces or free kicks in his career. He's fifth on the list with 65 goals and still going strong. Like CR7, he could end up right on top of this list before he retires from the game.
4. An Argentine midfielder has more free kick goals in his career than both Maradona and Messi. Retired Víctor Legrotaglie is not a famous name.

He ignored big club offers from Real Madrid and Inter Milan to spend his entire playing career at local side Gimnasia in his home city of Mendoza. Legrotaglie has an impressive 66 career goals from free kicks.

3. Third on the list is Brazilian legend Ronaldinho with 68 free kick goals, who dazzled with his skills in teams like Brazil, Barcelona, and AC Milan.
2. The greatest Brazilian to play the game and arguably the best footballer to grace the planet, Pelé finds a place on the list in second place with 70 goals scored from free kicks. Pelé has a staggering total of 1,279 goals in 1,363 matches.
1. It is a Brazilian who tops the list when it comes to taking free kicks. Juninho Pernambucano might come as a surprise name to many, but he was a great ball-striking specialist who has 77 goals from free kicks in his career for clubs like Vasco de Gama and Lyon. Only Messi or Cristiano Ronaldo can hope to dethrone Juninho from his throne at the top of this list. Time will tell!

Law 14: THE PENALTY KICK

The referee awards a penalty kick to the team whose player is fouled within the penalty area of the opposing team. In a penalty kick, the player has to beat only the goalkeeper by shooting from a specified spot to score a goal.

Euro 1976 was the first major international tournament to be decided by penalties when Czechoslovakia beat Germany 5–3 on penalties. Before this, drawn matches were decided by coin tosses or the drawing of straws. Can you imagine Messi and Mbappé drawing straws after a goalless World Cup final? Thank God for penalties.

Strange but True Facts about Penalties

- Football research indicates that some countries are better at taking penalties than others. Among the European nations, Belgium has the best penalty shoot-out record at an unbelievable 100 per cent. Too bad Belgium chokes when it comes to winning major tournaments. Germany has a penalty shoot-out win percentage of 71 per cent followed by France (50 per cent), Italy and Spain (33 per cent) and England (17 per cent). The bigger teams have more experienced players who can handle pressure better and are better penalty takers.
- Stats also indicate that right-footed players have had more success in converting penalties with a 76 per cent conversion rate than left-footed players (73 per cent success rate). But penalty shoot-outs from the last 20 years show a drop in the success of left-footed players to 58 per cent while for right-footers it has remained over 70 per cent.
- The harder a penalty is hit, the greater has been the conversion rate.
- It is possible for goalkeepers to distract penalty takers and save the penalty. Goalkeepers use different techniques to unsettle the penalty taker and try to psych him out by doing stuff like staring at him, talking to him, pushing the ball away, and spreading

themselves out to make themselves appear bigger than they are. Another tactic is to stand 6 to 10 cm off the centre of the goal either left or right marginally to make one side of the goal 2.9 per cent wider. Almost 60 per cent of the time, the penalty taker shoots towards the slightly larger side of the goal.

A research of 129 penalties taken during World Cup finals and the finals of the UEFA Champions League reveal the following data:

Power of Shot	Scored	Missed Target	Saved
50 per cent	47 per cent	0 per cent	53 per cent
75 per cent	81 per cent	1 per cent	18 per cent
100 per cent	63 per cent	31 per cent	7 per cent

However, research has also revealed that the penalty struck at 75 per cent of maximum power is the most successful one. Experts conclude that a combination of power and placement is the best way to take a penalty.

Law 15: THE THROW-IN

A throw-in is given after the ball has gone out of play, and it brings the ball back into play. It is given to the opponents of the player who last touched the ball before it went out of play.

Rules of the throw-in:

- The throw-in is made from where the ball left the field.
- The throw-in is given to the team who hasn't touched the ball last before it went off the field.
- The thrower must be looking at the field of play.
- The thrower has to stand with both feet planted on the ground on or outside the touchline.
- Both hands must be used to throw the ball from behind and over the head.
- The opposition players must stand at least 2 m away from the thrower.

Cool Throw-In Facts

- The best throw-in technique is to throw the ball at an angle of about 30 degrees to reach the maximum distance if you are opting for a long throw-in.
- Roy Delap, former midfielder of Stoke City, was famous for his long throw-ins, which led to many goals for his team.
- Former Swiss defender Christian Schwegler of FC Red Bull Salzburg was also known for his long throw-in ability.
- The longest throw-in was 51.33 m by Thomas Grønnemark of Denmark on 18 June 2010. It was a flip throw-in.

Law 16: THE GOAL KICK

A goal kick is given when the ball crosses the goal line, either on the ground or in the air, having last touched a member of the attacking side and without a goal being scored. The ball is given to the goalkeeper in such a case to take a goal kick.

Longest Range Goal in Football History

The most outrageous goal kick was scored by Argentine goalkeeper Leandro Requena for his club Cobresal in a 3–1 win over Colo-Colo in Chile's top football league. In the 77th minute, with his side leading 2–0, Requena took a customary goal kick that was longer than usual. The ball bounced over Colo-Colo goalkeeper Brayan Cortés, who was standing well outside his penalty area. He watched in despair as the ball bounced over his head and headed towards goal. Much to the amusement of the Cobresal fans, and to add to the embarrassment, Cortés stumbled as he tried in vain to chase the ball and stop it. But it crossed the line. TNT Sports Chile reported that the goal was scored from a distance of 101 m, and if this is true and ratified by Guinness World Records, it could break the record for the longest range goal in the history of football. The current record is 96.01 m, and this was achieved in 2021 by Tom King in a match between Newport County and Cheltenham Town in England's Football League Fourth Division. These are the moments when goalkeepers boast that the goal was not an accident but scored with intent and skill.

THE 3–2 SET-UP

Since the new rules have been adapted in football, the 3–2 set-up has become one of the most common goal kick structures. The 3–2 set-up is made up of the goalkeeper, the two centre backs and the two central midfielders of a team. The centre backs split up to create the back three along with the goalkeeper by traditionally positioning themselves close to the byline. The double pivot is when they normally position themselves behind the opposition's first line of attack. The centre backs or the full backs who are not included within the 3–2 system quantitatively can then have the freedom to move up into higher attacking positions, normally onto different horizontal lines to the double pivot. The 3–2 system is reflective of the increasing role of the goalkeeper in modern football, which is a total transformation from the earlier days when he was expected only to defend the goal. Today, goalkeepers are expected to use their feet as much as their hands and play the role of an extra defender. One of the main advantages of this set-up or system is that two midfielders can operate centrally, immediately behind the first line of attack. This makes both the midfield and the attack stronger, and there are more options to pass the ball from the first line of attack or the back three in the two full backs and the goalkeeper to the second line of attack or the double pivot. This strategy makes life tough for the defenders of the opponent team as more options are created to pass the ball from the central position. In the EPL and the Champions League, Pep Guardiola has successfully implemented this goal structure, which has contributed greatly to Manchester City's success. Teams like Manchester United in the EPL, AC Milan in Serie A, and RB Leipzig in the Bundesliga are some of the other teams that have used the 3–2 set-up throughout their season.

Law 17: THE CORNER KICK

A corner kick is given when the ball crosses the goal line, whether in the air or on the ground, having last touched a defender or the goalkeeper without a goal having been scored. It is also possible to score a goal directly from a corner kick, although the chances of that happening are very slim.

Key Corner Kick Facts

- The corner kick rule was introduced nine years after all the other original football laws were founded. Corners first came into play in football in 1872, and they have been an integral part of the game ever since. But the rules regarding the corner kick have constantly evolved over time along with the evolution of the game.
- A corner kick is awarded in football when the ball goes out of play via the end touchline, having last touched a player of the defending team without entering the goal. Unlike throw-ins, corner kicks are not taken from the spot from where the ball exited the field of play. Instead, corners are taken from the two corners of the pitch where the corner flags designate the precise spot from where the corner has to be taken.
- The ball is required to be stationary when a corner is taken in the form of a kick by a player of the attacking team from within the markings of the corner area or arc.
- A short corner is when the ball is passed quickly to a player close to the corner taker to mount a surprise

Corner Kick

attack. Otherwise, most corners are in the form of aerial balls directed towards the penalty area, where the attackers try to head the ball in and the defenders try to stop them from doing so.

Some of the Best Corner Takers in Football

There are some players who are regarded as the best corner takers or corner specialists as they have mastered the art of delivering the ball precisely where they want to. Their skill and ability to deliver deadly crosses that prove effective in getting a goal from their corner kicks is what makes them special players.

David Beckham (England, Manchester United, Real Madrid)

Just like his passes were delivered with pinpoint accuracy, the English midfielder David Beckham was equally effective with his potent free kicks and corner kicks. Thanks to his brilliant corner kicks that curled in perfectly, Manchester United snatched victory from the jaws of defeat in the iconic 1999 Champions League final against Bayern Munich. Beckham's last-minute corner was converted by Ole Gunnar Solsjkær in what was a thrilling and historic moment in football.

Andrea Pirlo (Italy, Juventus)

Italian legend Andrea Pirlo was an absolute master when it came to corner kicks with his fantastic dead ball ability. The playmaker swung in perfect balls from the corner kick, and he could not only make the football swerve and dip but also swing it in any direction he chose. That is called making a football talk.

Trent Alexander-Arnold (England, Liverpool)

The right back has been a consistent corner kick taker for his club side Liverpool, as well as for England. Despite his young age, he has notched up 13 assists from his corners and is considered one of the best exponents of corner kicks in modern football. His excellent corner against Barcelona in Liverpool's famous 2019 Champions League semi-final win is one of his greatest moments in his Liverpool jersey.

Xavi Hernández (Spain, Barcelona)

In his illustrious career for both club and country, Xavi Hernández has won the World Cup, the European Championship, the Champions League and La Liga. But some of Xavi's best moments on the pitch came from his corner kicks. His wide range of corners created numerous goal-scoring opportunities, and the best one is probably the one he curled in for Carles Puyol to head home against Germany in the semi-final of the 2010 World Cup. That goal was absolutely crucial for Spain to reach the World Cup final.

Can You Score a Goal Directly on a Corner Kick?

It is extremely difficult and rare to score a goal directly from a corner kick because of the angle involved. Even the best players cannot claim to have intentionally scored a goal through a corner kick. However, to do this, one must produce an in-swinging corner that has to beat the defenders as well as the goalkeeper and go directly into the

LA Galaxy v Chicago Fire, MLS 2011 | David Beckham's Corner Kick Leads LA Galaxy to a 2–1 Victory goal. The corner taker has to curl the ball using the inside of the foot to direct it towards the far corner of the net. This has been achieved on several occasions in football. Among the ones to pull off this almost impossible feat is German star Toni Kroos, who scored one against Valencia for Real Madrid in the Spanish Super Cup semi-final. David Beckham has done it for LA Galaxy in the MLS, and Brazilian set piece master Roberto Carlos did it for Corinthians in 2010.

LAWLESSNESS IN FOOTBALL

Why Laws Are Important

The lawlessness that prevailed in Colombian football for a very long time perfectly illustrates why laws are needed in football. In the 1980s and 1990s, football thrived in the South American country of Colombia thanks to the drug trade run by drug lords like cocaine kingpin Pablo Escobar. Through his drug operations and money laundering schemes, Escobar pumped a lot of money into Colombian football. During this phase, the game flourished in Colombia and enjoyed a golden period. No one complained as long as the team was winning, and herein was the error. Escobar laundered money by sponsoring a football team called Atlético Nacional, which soon became one of Colombia's premier professional teams. The huge inflow of cash attracted the top coaches and players to Colombian football, who received astronomical salaries. Slowly, as many as six professional Colombian clubs grew links with drug cartels that took control of Colombian football. The drug lords could now legitimize their illegal dealings thanks to football and also receive public support for their actions as the game was loved by everyone. But the dark side surfaced soon as briberies, kidnappings, and killings followed since betting on football was huge money now. Rival drug lord Miguel Rodríguez Orejuela heading the Cali cartel had acquired América de Cali, a premier league Colombian team. But even dirty money showed results as Colombia qualified for three FIFA World Cups in a row from 1990 to 1998 after a 28-year absence from football's biggest international tournament.

In 1989, a Colombian referee named Álvaro Ortega, officiating in the Categoría Primera A, was shot dead because he overruled a goal, enabling Amèrica de Cali to tie Independiente Medellín, which caused the murderous betters to lose a lot of money.

In 1994, the Colombian squad for the FIFA World Cup was its best ever. They had thumped Argentina 5–0 in qualifying and topped their group in South America. Brazilian legend Pelé predicted that Colombia would win the World Cup. But the sins were catching up as Colombia lost to the USA 2–1 in the opening round, with defender Andrés Escobar scoring an own goal. Colombia was eliminated from the group stage of the World Cup. But no one, not even Pelé, could have predicted what happened next. Andrés Escobar was shot dead outside a Colombian nightclub just a week later for scoring that own goal. Gloom descended all over Colombia, and football lovers across the world condemned this dastardly act. Escobar (no relation to the drug lord, of course) had been rumoured to join AC Milan after the World Cup to begin a promising career. Over 1,20,000 people attended Escobar's funeral, and they were all very angry.

Escobar's murder ended the narco-soccer period in Colombian football as authorities cracked down heavily on the drug lords. Sadly, Colombia's international football ranking plummeted from 4 to 34 without drug money. Colombia exited in the group stages of the 1998 FIFA World Cup again and failed to qualify after that for a long time. But good things take time and Colombian soccer soon saw a resurgence and an honest one at that. In 2014, Colombia reached the quarter-finals of the FIFA World Cup for the first time, and their star striker, James Rodríguez, won the Golden Boot award as the leading scorer of the tournament. Today, Colombia is again a potent force in South American and world football. Say no to drugs and drug money, and say yes to football is the new Colombian mantra.

The Truth behind the Murder of Andrés Escobar | The Nexus of Colombian Drugs and Football

2

ORIGINS, EVOLUTION AND FIRSTS

Origin of Football

Football originated in China during the Huan Dynasty as the Chinese sport called cuju. During the reign of the Asuka dynasty in Japan, a similar game was played called kemari. But the modern form of football, also known as association football, was developed in England in 1863.

The Cuju Ball

The Chinese sport cuju, which means 'to hit the ball with the foot', was played somewhere between 320 BCE and 500 BCE. It was a popular game among Chinese soldiers. The cuju balls were earlier made of two pieces of leather stitched together and filled inside with feathers. Later on, the ball was developed into 12 pieces of leather precisely sewn together, covering an inflatable animal bladder.

The Transformation of the Football

The Chinese footballs were created from sewn clothing that was filled with rubble. Footballs in the Middle Ages were made from inflated pig bladders. Today, the outer surface of the ball is composed of synthetic leather and the bladders inside the ball are made from latex or butyl.

Ban by English Royalty

Football spread to England in the 12th century. But in 1314, King Edward II banned the sport because of a military reason. The ban was continued by Richard II, Henry IV, Henry VIII and Elizabeth I. People playing football were jailed for a week. But despite this, football's popularity soared.

The First Games

The first games of football in England were played with a leather ball. A hole was created in a piece of silk cloth, and the players had to kick the ball through this hole to score a goal. In another version, the players ran with the ball in their hands to score a goal.

Complicated Rules

In another complicated format of the sport, the ball was tied to canes and hung at a height of approximately 9 m above the ground, where the players had to kick it with their feet.

The Single Goalpost

To make life easier and ensure that more goals were scored, several variations were made to the original game as the new format spread towards Asia. The most prominent one was a goalpost placed bang in the middle of the field.

Introduction of Two Goalposts

As the modern version of the sport started gaining in popularity, the solitary goalpost in the middle of the field was replaced by proper football goalposts introduced on each side of the field.

Origin of the Name Football

Football received its name not because the ball is supposed to be kicked by the foot in this sport. It was named so because the sport was played on foot. In earlier times, people with a higher social status played sports on horseback, while peasants played sports on foot.

The First Football Games in England

In England, the first competitive games were played between neighbouring villages and towns. An animal bladder was used for a ball, and particular areas like the church or a village square served as the area to be reached for one particular team to score a goal.

Mob Football

The earliest football games played in England with an inflated animal bladder barely had any rules. Rules were also difficult to impose as there were no restrictions on how many players could participate in the game. Such games were known as 'mob football'.

Transformation of Mob Football

The credit for the transformation of 'mob football' to 'regular football' goes to the public schools of Britain. These schools formed some basic rules that the players participating in the sport would have to follow. Matches with these rules in place were first played between several schools.

Rules of Football

The first rules of 'football' were formulated by the Rugby School (1845), which permitted the use of hands, followed by the Eton rules (1847), which advocated much more restricted handling of the ball. As the uniquely created rules of each school led to chaos that prevented competition between teams due to the lack of a unifying code, representatives from the schools with football teams convened at Cambridge University in 1848. They founded the first standardized football game, known as the 'Cambridge Rules', agreeing on a common set of regulations. These new rules stipulated that players could only kick the ball with their feet, with only the goalkeeper allowed to handle the ball, and that players on the same team must wear uniforms of the same colour.

The first universal laws of football were drawn up in 1863 in England. Subsequently, the International Football

Association Board (IFAB) was formed in Britain in 1886 to develop and protect these rules all over the world.

The World's First Football Club

The first football club in the world was formed in 1857. Two British army officers named Colonel Nathaniel Creswick and Major William Priest were the co-founders of the English Sheffield Football Club. The club currently plays in the Northern Premier League Division One South East.

The FA Cup

The FA Cup was the world's first football competition and exists to date. The first FA Cup was held in London in the year 1871.

Sheffield FC, Dronfield, Derbyshire, England

First International Match

The first international football game that was recognized by FIFA took place on 30 November 1872 at Hamilton Crescent between Scotland and England. The match was a goalless draw, and 114 games have been played since then between the two national teams.

Soccer

Football is known as soccer in the USA, Canada and Australia. That's because all three nations have their own version of football as well in American football, Canadian football, and Australian rules football.

Origin of the Term 'Soccer'

Strangely, the term 'soccer' originated in England. During the 19th century, it was considered fashionable in England to add the '-er' sound to any shortened word. The term 'Association Football' was also shortened to 'Assoc Football', which was again shortened to the term 'soccer'.

The First Televised Football Match

The first live coverage of a football game on television took place in 1937 by the BBC. This was, however, a practice game played at Highbury Stadium between the main Arsenal team and the Arsenal Reserves.

Highest Attendance

The highest attendance in a football match was recorded at the Maracanã Stadium in 1950, where 1,73,850 people gathered to watch Uruguay play Brazil.

Television Broadcast

In 1937, the first football game was televised in the U.K. The first game that was broadcast in colour was 30 years later, in 1967.

Football in South America

Football is called 'fútbol' in Spanish and known as 'futebol' in Portuguese. The sport arrived in Latin America in the late 1800s, and since then, has been deeply embedded in the identity and culture of South America. The Copa America tournament decides the champions of South America.

The First South American Football Club

Football arrived in South America in the 19th century in Argentina. European sailors introduced the game in the port of Buenos Aires. In 1867, the British people in the area formed the first club, named the Buenos Aires Football Club. Soon, British railway workers started another club in Rosario, Argentina.

The First Argentinean League Championship

In 1893, the first league championship was held in Argentina. But most of the players hailed from the British community, and this trend of no local players continued till the early 20th century.

Football Arrives in Brazil

The second South American country that witnessed the invasion of football was reportedly Brazil. In 1894, a leading English player arrived in Brazil and introduced the game of football in the city of São Paulo. The athletic club of São Paulo was the first one to start playing professional football.

Football Invades Uruguay and Colombia

In 1891, British railway workers in Uruguay formed the Central Uruguay Railway Cricket Club, now famously known as Peñarol, which played both cricket and football. British engineers and workers engaged in building a railroad near Barranquilla, Colombia, introduced the sport there and the Barranquilla FBC was founded in 1909.

Football in Chile and Bolivia

In 1891, British sailors introduced the sport in Chile as the Valparaíso FC was founded in 1889 in the town of the same name. Chilean students who had studied in Europe were the first footballers in Bolivia, while expatriate Britons introduced football in Peru.

Football in Paraguay

In Paraguay, Dutchman William Paats introduced football at a school where he taught physical education. But the first Paraguayan football club, Olimpia, was formed by a local who fell in love with the sport after watching a match in Buenos Aires in 1902.

Football Spreads across the South American Continent

British miners in Venezuela, on the other hand, had been playing football there since the 1880s. Slowly but steadily, football spread to all corners of South America to become the region's most popular sport. Little boys passionately played the game on abandoned as well as crowded streets.

The Arrival of Black Players

Vasco da Gama won the league championship in 1923 thanks to its Black recruits, prompting other South American clubs to follow the leader as more and more Black players started playing professional football in South America.

South American Export to Europe

After the first World Cup in 1930, which was hosted and won by Uruguay, there was an exodus of South American

Vasco da Gama Football Club Flag

footballers to play in European clubs, enticed by higher salaries. The number has risen steadily along with the salaries over the years.

Football Becomes Part of South American Culture

By the late 1930s, football had become an integral part of popular culture in several South American countries. Black players began their struggle to participate at the topmost level. Their efforts bore fruit when Rio de Janeiro club Vasco da Gama became the first club to recruit talented Black players.

Uruguay's Style of Football

Uruguay was mostly composed of people with mixed European descent. Hence, Uruguayan footballers picked up the physical playing style of the English, as well as the refined passing game of the Scottish players. This created a versatile style that helped Uruguay win two Olympic Championships and the first World Cup.

Football Arrives in Africa

In the second half of the 19th century, football entered the African continent thanks to European sailors, soldiers, traders, engineers and missionaries. In 1862, Cape Town in South Africa hosted the first documented match in Africa. It didn't take long for football to spread its wings throughout Africa after that.

The Early African Tournaments

The North African Championship was established in 1919 as teams from Algeria, Morocco and Tunisia competed with each other. Kenya and Uganda first played for the Gossage Trophy in 1924, south of the Sahara Desert. In 1925, a football league for Africans began in the Congo, and the North African Cup was introduced in 1930.

Football in South Africa

Football was always popular in South Africa with the first documented football match being played there. But because of the apartheid policy of the regime, football was divided into racially segregated groups of associations as the whites, Africans and coloureds (people of mixed race) played separately.

The Spread of Football in Africa

Two British African colonies launched their own football associations. The first was the Gold Coast in 1922, which is now known as Ghana. Nigeria followed suit in 1931. In the 1930s, French West Africa witnessed a footballing boom with clubs and leagues mushrooming, especially in Senegal and Côte d'Ivoire.

The First African to Play in Europe

Moroccan striker Larbi Ben Barek became the first African professional footballer to play in Europe. He was a member of the French club Olympique de Marseille and also became a member of the French national football team in 1938.

African Football after World War II

Post World War II, African football grew by leaps and bounds. New facilities were created by the colonial regimes that began bigger competitions like the French West Africa Cup in 1947. More African players migrated to play for European clubs. Great footballers like Mário Coluna and Mozambican superstar Eusébio arrived on the scene.

Combining Football and Nationalism

Algerian stars Rachid Mekhloufi of Saint-Étienne and Mustapha Zitouni of AS Monaco also represented France. In 1958, they joined the football team of the Algerian National Liberation Front (FLN). The FLN team lost only 4 of the 58 matches they played during 1958–62. The team portrayed the affinity between nationalist movements and football in Africa's colonial period.

Africa Breaks Free

As Africa broke free from the shackles of colonialism, the Confédération Africaine de Football (CAF) was established in Khartoum, Sudan in February 1957. The first African Cup of Nations tournament also began during the same period.

Postcolonial African Football

Postcolonial Africa witnessed the emergence of a signature style in African football in the 1960s and early '70s. A grand, attacking style of play made African football immensely popular. Salif Keïta (Mali), Laurent Pokou (Côte d'Ivoire), and François M'Pelé (Congo) were the popular footballers in early postcolonial Africa.

The Indomitable Lions

In the 1980s and '90s, the Indomitable Lions, as Cameroon's national team was known, was largely responsible for making African football famous all over the world. True to their name, the Lions exited the 1982 World Cup with heads held high and without losing a single match. They also drew with Italy.

The Lions Stun the Giants

In the 1990 World Cup, Cameroon stunned defending champions and Diego Maradona–led Argentina in the opening match and went on to reach the quarter-finals. Africa's golden moment had arrived! Nigeria continued

Indomitable Lions Team Logo

the good work by winning the Olympic gold medal in men's football at the Summer Games in Atlanta in 1996.

Golden Moments of African Football

In 2000, Cameroon won its first Olympic gold medal in men's football. The youth football teams of Nigeria won the under-17 title in 1985. The feat was repeated by Ghana in 1991 and 1995. Then, in 1995, Liberian striker George Weah of PSG received the prestigious FIFA World Player of the Year award.

Football Rolls into Asia and Oceania

At the end of the 19th century, football rolled into Asia and Oceania. But unlike Europe and South America, it failed to be the No. 1 sport there. Australian rules football was still the most popular sport in Australia. In New Zealand, rugby remained a national passion.

Football in Asia

In Asia, football was extremely popular in Calcutta (now Kolkata) thanks to the British soldiers. But locals adapted to cricket in India more than football. The Japanese cities of Yokohama and Kobe saw an influx of foreign footballers, but the Japanese initially preferred the traditional sport of sumo wrestling and baseball, which was imported from America.

Football as a Symbol of Asian Culture

The 21st century saw football become a part of the culture and politics of several Asian countries. In Iran, national team football matches led to the expression of reformist political views and unified mass celebration. When the Iraqi football team won fourth place at the 2004 Olympics, they were a symbol of hope for their war-torn nation.

The AFC

The Asian Football Confederation (AFC) helms the footballing affairs in Asia. The Asian Cup began in 1956 with Iran, Saudi Arabia, Japan and South Korea dominating over the years to date.

The J.League

Club football in Asia was further enhanced thanks to rapid economic growth during the 1980s and early 1990s. Japan profited especially with regard to club football development thanks to cultural and trade tie-ups with the West as the J.League was formed in 1993.

The Rise of Japanese Football

The arrival of foreign players and coaches in the J.league, with the likes of Brazilian Zico, greatly improved the standard of Japanese football. Public interest in the sport also catapulted, and today, after years of hard work, Japan is a force to reckon with in world football.

Asian Success at the World Cup

Asian success at the international level came in 1966 when North Korea upset Italy at the World Cup. In 1994, Saudi Arabia became the first Asian team to qualify for the second round of the World Cup. In the 2022 World Cup,

Saudi Arabia convincingly defeated eventual champions Argentina.

Asia Shines Bright

Asian football was considerably boosted when South Korea and Japan co-hosted the 2002 World Cup. Japan reached the second round while South Korea reached the semi-finals of the tournament. Asian football had truly arrived on the world scene. Japan and South Korea were also the surprise packages of the 2022 World Cup.

Most Expensive Footballer of All Time

Brazilian superstar Neymar Jr. was involved in a world-record transfer move to PSG from Barcelona in 2017. The 222 million transfer fee was almost double the earlier record fee. Neymar Jr. became the most expensive footballer in history by a long shot.

3

AMAZING BUT TRUE!

Goalkeeper Jerseys

In the beginning, the only distinguishable feature for goalkeepers was a flat cap. It was in 1909 that the FA decided that goalkeepers will be wearing a different coloured jersey than their teammates, but only red, white and blue were allowed till 1990 (until green was permitted). Before that, goalies wore the same jersey as their teammates, but this was changed because of the occasional confusion it caused in the goalmouth for the officials.

Playing Basketball with a Football

The first games of basketball were played using a football or a soccer ball. It was only later that the proper basketball came into existence.

Unconscious Physio

In 1930, a physiotherapist from the USA team treated an injured player on the pitch. He lost his footing and landed on a bottle of chloroform that slipped out of his pocket. The physio lost consciousness, and both he and the player had to be led out on stretchers.

Longest to Play a World Cup

Two countries participated in the World Cup together as early as 1938. Cuba and Indonesia have not been able to qualify for any other World Cup after that. That means it's been 86 years since they have played in a World Cup game. That's a tournament record in failure to qualify.

16 Goals in a Game

In December 1942, a French footballer named Stéphan Stanis scored as many as 16 goals for Racing Club de Lens in a wartime French Cup game. This bizarre record hasn't been broken for as long as 82 years!

Going the Distance

The average distance covered by a football player during a football game is roughly 7–10 miles, that is almost 11–16 km in 90 minutes.

Lucky Escape

The 1956 Cup Final in England took place between Manchester City and Birmingham City. A footballer named Bert Trautmann broke his neck during the match and was knocked out. He was revived and continued playing. No one realized then that he had suffered such a serious neck injury.

Peru Riots

In 1964, a football match in Peru resulted in a riot that killed over 300 people and injured more than 500 people because of a referee's erroneous call in the game.

Football Ceasefire

In 1967, the two warring factions in the Nigerian Civil War decided to go on a ceasefire for 48 hours. There was no fighting so that both sides could watch legendary football player Pelé play in an exhibition match in Lagos.

War over Football

In 1969, El Salvador went to war against Honduras after losing a controversial football match. This is the first and only instance of two countries going to war over a football match.

Most Goals in a Match

In a bizarre football match in Madagascar, a total of 149 goals were scored for the final scoreline to be 149–0 in favour of AS Adema.

SO l'Emyrne lost the game intentionally to protest against an unfair decision taken by the referee in a previous game.

Camus's Dream

The famous philosopher Albert Camus played as a goalkeeper for his university football team. Camus loved football but had to abandon his dream of being a professional footballer after being diagnosed with tuberculosis. Football's loss is philosophy's gain!

Celebration Injuries

Approximately more than one in 20 injuries sustained during a football match are because of celebrating on the pitch after scoring a goal. Beware of diving celebrations after a goal has been scored!

Bend It Like the Men

In England, women started playing football around the same time as men. But women's football was banned in 1921 and only reinstated in 1971 officially. It became popular in the 1990s, and the women's football league is known as the FA Women's National League.

Unity in Sleeves

English Premier League Club Arsenal has a tradition where the team captain gets to choose the length of the team's T-shirt sleeves. This is reflective of the team's unity by wearing the same-sized T-shirt sleeves. Gunners are all the same after all!

No Football on the Moon

When astronaut Neil Armstrong went to the moon, he wanted to take a football along with him. But his proposal was rejected by NASA because of a strange reason. They felt the act was too un-American.

Club versus Country

South Korean footballer Ahn Jung-hwan was removed from his Italian club Perugia in Serie A. The bizarre reason for his exclusion from his club team was that he scored the winning goal in the 2002 World Cup while playing for South Korea to knock out the Italian football team. Bad losers!

Going Dutch

The football team with the longest name in the world has 83 letters. The name of the Dutch team is Nooit Opgeven Altijd Doorzetten Aangenaam Door Vermaak En Nuttig Door Ontspanning Combinatie Breda. Thankfully, they are referred to as NAC Breda.

Too Much Nylon Twine

At White Heart Lane, the former stadium of EPL club Tottenham Hotspurs, nylon twine is used to stitch all the grass together on the football field. There is so much twine in this stadium that it can be stretched across the world! Now, that's a lot of twine.

Playing for Three Countries

The only footballer to have the unique distinction of playing for as many as three different countries recognized by FIFA is László Kubala. He represented Argentina, Spain, and Columbia.

Oldest Footballer

The oldest living footballer is Japanese Kazuyoshi Miura. Miura is 57 years old and plays for Yokohama FC in the

Japanese League, and is currently on loan to club Atletico Suzuka. He has been playing professional football since he was just 15.

Two Is Not a Crowd

The Isles of Scilly boasts of the unique feat of having just two football teams: the Woolpack Wanderers and Garrison Gunners. These two teams play each other every week. It must be a tad boring for the local spectators of the sport!

Goalkeeper Turned Author

Sir Arthur Conan Doyle, the famous creator of Sherlock Holmes, was the goalkeeper for English club Portsmouth under the name A.C. Smith.

Kazuyoshi Miura's Wax Statue, Madame Tussauds Museum, Odaiba, Japan

Made in Pakistan

80 per cent of the footballs used across the world in professional football are manufactured in Pakistan. Since 1982, Sialkot in Pakistan has been making the footballs for the FIFA World Cup. They are hand-stitched to make high-quality footballs.

Two Matches in a Day

If playing one football match in a day wasn't stressful enough, Mark Hughes had to play two football matches in a single day for his club and his country. On 11 November 1987, Hughes played 2 matches for Wales and Bayern Munich on the same day.

You Win Some and You Lose Some

In the morning, Mark Hughes represented Wales against Czechoslovakia in Prague in a European qualifier. Wales lost this match, and Hughes drove across the border to play for Bayern Munich in the afternoon in a Cup clash with Borussia Mönchengladbach. Hughes must have sighed when Bayern Munich won.

Smart Goalkeeping

Simon Mignolet, the goalkeeper of Liverpool, was armed with a degree in politics and spoke five languages. But he only became a goalkeeper after he was dropped from the team while playing as a forward. That's forward thinking!

The Non-Flying Dutchman

Arsenal legend Dennis Bergkamp missed many away games of his club because of his fear of flying. He was nicknamed the Non-Flying Dutchman by Arsenal fans.

Scoring in Every Minute

Cristiano Ronaldo was the first footballer to score a goal in every minute of a 90-minute football game in his career, scoring most frequently in the 23rd minute of games. Zlatan Ibrahimović was the second footballer to achieve this unique feat in his career.

Footballer Turned Celebrity Chef

Gordon Ramsay is one of the most famous celebrity chefs in the world. But he was a promising footballer in his younger days and was scouted by Rangers. However, he had to abandon his plans of being a professional footballer after suffering a knee injury.

Forgetful Referee

Referee Michel Vautrot added 8 minutes in the first period of extra time in the 1990 World Cup semi-final between Italy and Argentina. After the match, it was revealed that he had simply lost track of time.

Struck by Lightning

In 1998, two villages in the Congo, Basangana and Bena Tshadi, were involved in a football match. Suddenly, a bolt of lightning struck the pitch, killing all eleven players of one team while the other team remained untouched.

Enter Ronaldinho

Brazilian superstar Ronaldinho first came into the limelight in 1988. His local youth team won 23–0 in a game in Porto Allegre, Brazil. A 13-year-old Ronaldinho scored all the 23 goals in the match.

Seventh Heaven

The largest football tournament in the world witnessed participation from over 5,098 teams. This was the 1999 League 7-a-side competition held in Bangkok, Thailand.

Seeing Red

A football game between General Caballero and Sportivo Ameliano in Paraguay turned especially ugly. As many as 20 red cards were shown in this match.

Largest Football Stadium

Not much is known about North Korea because of its totalitarian regime and closed economy. But the North Korean capital is home to the largest football stadium. The Rungrado 1st of May Stadium in Pyongyang has a capacity of almost 1,50,000 people. Some sources claim the capacity is 1,14,000, which still makes it the largest stadium worldwide.

Stadium 974, Qatar

Stadium 974

The latest World Cup hosted by Qatar saw a 'transportable' stadium host several matches. Stadium 974 is made of shipping containers and is the world's first fully demountable football venue with a capacity of 40,000.

Transfer Fees Paid in Footballs

The Argentinian star footballer Ángel Di María helped his side to World Cup glory in Qatar and is one of the richest footballers. But in his younger days, Di María was traded between two of his homeland football clubs for just 35 footballs.

Undefeated by Brazil

Brazil is arguably the greatest team in the history of football in terms of performance. But there is one country in the world that the great Brazilian team has never defeated. Norway has played 4 matches against Brazil and has beaten Brazil twice with 2 matches drawn.

Same Size of the Ball

Football has experienced numerous changes over the years. Every World Cup, something new is introduced in terms of rules and/or technology. But one thing that has remained constant over the years is the size of the football. For 120 years, the football still has a circumference of 28 inches.

Fighting at Fifty

In 2004, Brazilian legend Socrates played a match for Garforth Town in the Northern Counties East Football League. He was 50 years old then and also the player–manager of Garforth Town when they played against Tadcaster Albion.

Longest Penalty Shoot-Out

2005 witnessed the longest penalty shoot-out in Namibia. KK Palace and Civics faced each other in the Namibian Cup, and it took 48 penalty kicks to decide the winner. This is also a Guinness World Record. The penalty shoot-out was as long as the game itself, and each player had to take 3 penalty kicks.

Most Red Cards

In 2011, arch-rivals Claypole and Victoriano Arenas in the 5th tier Argentinean football league faced each other. In the first half, two players received the red card. But in the second half, a total of 36 red cards were shown. Referee Damián Rubino red-carded all twenty-two players players and fourteen substitutes and coaches.

The Swedish Legend

Swedish footballer Zlatan Ibrahimović became a star when he was playing in his youth team. When his team was 4–0 down, Zlatan came in as a substitute and won the match for his team by scoring 8 goals.

Age Difference

The age difference between Lionel Messi and Christiano Ronaldo is 869 days. Interestingly, this difference is the same as the age difference between Messi's son and Ronaldo's son. Perhaps we shall see two more superstars in world football in the coming years.

Always on the Winning Side

Zinedine Zidane has scored many goals during his illustrious career for both his club and country. But the amazing fact is that Zidane has won almost everything, including the World Cup, Champions League, Ballon d'Or, and a number of domestic titles. But the Copa del Rey remains elusive, both as a player and manager.

Pelé the Great

Brazilian legend Pelé's footballing resume is certainly impressive. Apart from winning a record three World Cups for Brazil, Pelé has 92 hat-tricks to his name. He has scored 4 goals on 31 occasions, 5 goals on six occasions, and 8 goals on one occasion. That's why he's considered the best ever.

No Grass in Greenland

When Greenland applied to FIFA to become a footballing nation, it found its application rejected. The reason for the rejection was that not enough grass grows in Greenland for it to have a proper football field. Well, the grass is always greener on the other side, particularly for Greenland.

Longest Football Match in India

The longest recorded football match in Indian football history was played in 2015 between two local teams from Goa, India, named FC Bardez and FC Salcete. They played for a total of 164 hours and 42 minutes, with the teams playing for 11 hours a day. That's a tough one to beat!

Youngest Player to Play World Cup Qualification

Souleymane Mamam of Togo is the youngest footballer to play in a World Cup qualifying match. He was 13 years and 310 days when he came in as a substitute three minutes from the final whistle to replace Komlan Assignon.

The Famous Five

As many as five asteroids have been named after five European football players, which is a huge honour. Here's the special list:

Football Player	Asteroid Name
Arsène Wenger	33179 Arsènewenger
Johan Cruyff	14282 Cruyff
Josef Bican	10634 Pepibican
Ferenc Puskás	82656 Puskás
Michael Ballack	79647 Ballack

Deadly Duo

When the two legendary Brazilian footballers Pelé and Garrincha played together, Brazil never lost a single game.

Named after Diego

Brazilian footballer Diego Costa was named in honour of Diego Maradona by his parents despite the intense footballing rivalry between Argentina and Brazil.

Two Nations

The first player to represent two different countries in World Cups was Luis Monti (Argentina 1930 and Italy 1934). The five other players are:

- Robert Prosinečki (Yugoslavia 1990, Croatia 1998)
- Robert Jarni (Yugoslavia 1990, Croatia 1998)
- José Santamaría (Uruguay 1954, Spain 1962)

- Ferenc (Hungary 1954, Spain 1962)
- Mazzola (Brazil 1958, Italy 1962)

Barcelona Passion

When Spanish footballer Xavi was 19 years old, he received an offer to join Milan. Xavi's father gave him permission, but his mother was furious. She told her husband that if Xavi was allowed to leave Barcelona, she would divorce him. As a result, Xavi stayed on in Barcelona.

Father and Son in a Team

Former Chelsea and Barcelona striker Eidur Smari Gudjohnsen made his international debut for Iceland when he was 17 years old. In the second half, the coach substituted him with his own father, Arnor Gudjohnsen, who was also in the national team. Father and son later complained that they were denied the chance to play together.

Belgian Baby

In a bizarre move that defies all explanation, a 20-month-old baby became the youngest professional football player ever, after being signed up by a Belgian club. Catch them young, we say!

Neuer's Acting Talent

Many footballers are good actors on the pitch, falling and pretending they were fouled. But referees kept a hawk-eye on German goalkeeper Manuel Neuer when everyone realized he had real acting talent. Neuer acted in an important part in the German version of *Monsters University*, the 2013 Pixar film.

Drogba for Peace

Famous Ivory Coast captain and ex-Chelsea football player Didier Drogba is credited with brokering a ceasefire in his home country. This ceasefire ended a five-year civil war in the Ivory Coast. Well played, Drogba!

Born at Sea

Former French player Rio Mavuba who had a long playing and coaching career at Bordeaux has a strange birth certificate. It does not have a nation listed in it and simply says 'Born at sea'. That's because Mavuba was born in international waters.

Fastest Red Card in Football

The fastest red card in football history was given to the former wide player for Newcastle United and Blackburn Rovers, Keith Gillespie, during the English Premier League in 2007. A throw-in was preceded by the substitution of Gillespie onto the pitch. Due to his impatience, Gillespie shoved Reading hardman Stephen Hunt in the face when he was vying for the throw-in. Even after being formally dismissed, he managed to give Hunt a shove in the face as he made his way to the tunnel. But it took 12 seconds for Gillespie to see red. The throw-in had not yet been made, and technically the referee had not restarted the game, and hence he got the red card at zero seconds.

The Strict Referee

As the referee whistled to signal the start of the game, the twenty-two-year-old Lee Todd whispered, 'F*ck me, ref, that was loud' and received the red card instantly. His teammates laughed as they thought it was a joke, but the referee was dead serious. Todd was also fined 27 pounds and banned for 35 days.

Crazy Transfer Window

In 1998, transfer windows reached a crazy level in England when footballer David Unsworth signed for both Aston Villa and Everton in the same summer. The most unethical part was that both the deals were only a month apart. The same season, Coventry signed Robert Jarni from Real Betis only to sell him to Real Madrid after four days.

Buffon's Longevity

Italian goalkeeper Gianluigi Buffon has certainly had a long footballing career. Buffon has played with or against six father-and-son duos – the Weahs, the Thurams, the Chiesas, the Simeones, the Valotis, and the Fricks. That's some career!

Most Goals in an Unrigged Football Match

The most team goals scored in a football match was in a game in Scotland in 1885. Arbroath defeated Bon Accord 36–0. The most goals in a match by an individual were scored by Archie Thompson for Australia against American

Samoa. In a 31–0 win for Australia, Thompson scored 13 goals.

Song's Twenty-Seven Siblings

Cameroonian midfielder Alex Song has played football for Arsenal and Barcelona. He has twenty-seven siblings – seventeen sisters and ten brothers! Song lost his father when he was three years old. His uncle, Rigobert Song, has been like his second father and was a major influence in Alex choosing football as a career.

King Uncle

Rigobert Song was himself a professional footballer and is the current manager of the Cameroon football team. He has played for clubs like West Ham and Liverpool apart from representing Cameroon.

Longest Unbeaten Streak

A football club remained undefeated for an astonishing 119 matches at a stretch. Romanian club Steaua Bucharest achieved this record of the longest unbeaten streak and also won five straight league titles and the 1985–86 European Cup.

Most Domestic League Titles

Glasgow Rangers is the most successful club in the world with respect to winning domestic league titles. The Rangers have won the Scottish Premiership a staggering 55 times.

The Ballon d'Or

The Ballon d'Or award is given to the best footballer in the world and has seen the topmost players win it. However, the coveted trophy has been won by European players 60 times out of the total 66 times it has been awarded.

Ballon d'Or Trophy

4

FIFA FEVER

FIFA WORLD CUP AMAZING FACTS

The Trophy

The World Cup trophy weighs 6.175 kilograms and is made of solid 18-carat gold. The official ball of the 2022

FIFA World Cup and the Official Adidas Al Rihla Ball

FIFA World Cup in Qatar was called the Adidas Al Rihla, and it is made up of 20 seamless panels.

The Only Eight

Only eight teams have won the FIFA World Cup in its entire history from 1930 to date. They are:

- Brazil: Five times
- Germany: Four times
- Italy: Four times
- Argentina: Thrice
- France: Twice
- Uruguay: Twice
- England: Once
- Spain: Once

What a View!

The FIFA World Cup is the most viewed sporting event in the world. 3.572 billion viewers watched the 2018 World Cup in Russia from across the world. That's the population of more than half the world. More than 265 million people in the world also play football.

Hat-Trick Is a No Trick

No team has won the World Cup three times in a row, but two teams have come rather close to achieving a hat-trick of World Cup titles. Italy won back-to-back World Cups in 1934 and 1938 but failed to win in the next event that only took place in 1950. Brazil won two straight World Cups in 1958 and 1962 but could not do so in 1966.

Continental Supremacy

Only European and South American nations have won the World Cup thus far. But Europe has a stronger record as any one European nation has always made it to the finals of all World Cups except two of them in the 90 years of the FIFA World Cup.

Global Broadcast

Although the 1952 World Cup in Switzerland was the first televised World Cup, Mexico 1970 witnessed the first global broadcast of the World Cup. Live television broadcast of World Cup action finally reached Antarctica during the 2010 World Cup in South Africa.

Klose to Goals

German footballer Miroslav Klose has scored the most goals in the World Cup. Klose has 16 goals to his name, which is 1 more than Brazilian great Ronaldo. That's some achievement as even the mercurial Pelé has only 12 World Cup goals to his credit.

Bergomi's Blues

Italian player Giuseppe Bergomi is a rarity for having represented the Azzurri in four World Cups. The amazing fact is that despite this impressive attendance, he has never played a single World Cup qualifier for Italy.

A Substitute Like No Other

Brazilian footballer Denilson is the most successful substitute in World Cup history. Denilson came on as a substitute 11 times in World Cups, including the two finals in the 1998 and 2002 World Cups.

Present Please

The crown of the No. 1 fan of professional football goes to Claudio Ribeiro of Brazil. He has never failed to attend a World Cup and cheer Brazil ever since the 1978 FIFA World Cup. Ribeiro has visited eleven countries to attend eleven World Cups. Of course, the list includes Brazil, which hosted the event in 2014.

To Brazil!

Brazil is the most successful team when it comes to winning World Cups. Brazil was champion of the world five times in 1958, 1962, 1970, 1994, and 2002. Brazil is also the only country that has qualified for and played all twenty-two editions of the World Cup!

Show Me the Money!

Apart from the glory of being champions of the world, the money is pretty good, too. The winning team of the World Cup gets $42 million while the runner-up receives $38 million. Even the teams that exit in the group stages make a cool $10 million. How's that for motivation?

So Close, Yet So Far

One feels bad for the Netherlands, though. Despite being a strong team in international football, the World Cup has always proved elusive for the Orange Army. The

Netherlands has the unique distinction of being the runner-up on three different occasions in the World Cup.

Girl Power

The first FIFA Women's World Cup was hosted by China in 1991 and has been held eight times since then. Four countries have won the Women's World Cup with the USA women's team being the most dominant force.

- USA: 4 titles
- Germany: 2 titles
- Norway: 1 title
- Japan: 1 title

Referable Referee

The referee officiating in the most matches in World Cups is Joël Quiniou from France. He has refereed 8 matches between 1986 and 1994, including four in USA '94.

Jan Langenus (1930), Nicolay Latyshev (1962), and José Ramiz Wright (1990) have also officiated in 4 games in one World Cup.

No Country Is Too Small to Play

Iceland is the country with the smallest population to have ever played in the World Cup. The population of this small nation is only 3,34,000.

Collecting Cards

French legend Zinedine Zidane and Brazilian star Cafu hold the dubious record for the most cards in World

Cups with six cautions each. The two players who have been sent off twice at a World Cup are Rigobert Song and Zinedine Zidane.

A Record Nevertheless

The World Cup record of conceding the most goals in the history of the World Cup is jointly held by two not-so-proud goalkeepers. Mexico's Antonio Carbajal and Saudi Arabia's Mohamed Al-Deayea have each let in 25 goals in World Cups.

Three Is the Charm

The upcoming 2026 FIFA World Cup will feature three host nations for the first time. Canada, Mexico, and the United States will jointly host the Cup. This will be the third time Mexico will host the World Cup after 1970 and 1986, becoming the only nation to do so.

The More the Merrier

Another interesting feature of the 2026 FIFA World Cup will be the change in format. Instead of the 32 teams that competed in the last World Cup in Qatar, there will be 48 international teams this time fighting for ultimate footballing honours. That's an addition of 16 teams.

Let's Play, Brother!

A total of five pairs of brothers have played in a World Cup final. But only two pairs of brothers emerged as champions: the Charlton (England, 1966) and the Walter brothers (West Germany, 1954). The brothers to lose

Marcos Evangelista de Morais aka Cafu

in the final were the Evaristo (Argentina, 1930), Van de Kerkhof (Netherlands, 1974–78) and Forster (West Germany, 1982).

Consistent Cafu

Brazilian defender Cafu has a unique achievement in the World Cup. He is the only player to have played in three consecutive World Cup finals in 1994, 1998, and 2002. Even the great Maradona managed only two in 1986 and 1990.

Zinedine Zidane's Headbutt on Marco Materazzi | Germany 2006 | FIFA World Cup

La Plage - Coup de Boule Song, 2006

Music from the Field

The famous song 'Coup de Boule' (headbutt) was inspired by Zinedine Zidane's legendary headbutt on Italian player Marco Materazzi in the final that probably cost France the World Cup in 2006. The French have a song for every occasion!

Smashed in the First

In the Women's FIFA World Cup, the record for the maximum goals in a single match belongs to the USA. They beat Thailand 13–0 in the inaugural game of the 2019 World Cup.

Double Hat-Trick

Four players have the unique record of scoring two hat-tricks at the World Cup. They are:

- Sandor Kocsis of Hungary in 1954
- Just Fontaine of France in 1958
- Gerd Müller of West Germany in 1970
- Gabriel Batistuta of Argentina scored one in 1994 and the other in 1998.

What the Stats Say

7.36 per cent of all goals that have been scored in World Cup history have come from the penalty shot, and 1.25 per cent have come as own goals. Now that's an interesting World Cup stat!

Early World Cup Facts: Before 1930

- Encouraged by the success of the football tournaments in the Olympic Games in 1924 and 1928, FIFA decided to launch the first FIFA World Cup in Uruguay in 1930. Uruguay was celebrating the 100th anniversary of its first constitution. Thirteen countries participated in the inaugural Football World Cup.

- Uruguay's National Football Association offered to pay all the costs of the travelling countries, including food, accommodation, and travel, and was given the rights to host the first World Cup. Uruguay was also Olympic champion in football in 1924 and 1928.
- Several countries refused to attend the inaugural World Cup because of the long journey to Uruguay. In 1930, travelling by sea was the only feasible option because commercial aviation began in the mid-50s. It was the first and last World Cup to have more South American teams than European teams.
- Travel was cumbersome, and only four European teams – Romania, France, Yugoslavia, and Belgium – travelled together on a single ship named SS *Conte Verde* on June 21. If that wasn't enough cost-cutting, they travelled across the Atlantic to pick up the Brazilian team from Rio before reaching Uruguay.
- Despite the fact that all associate teams were invited to play and the tournament didn't have a qualifying process, many European teams did not attend. The travelling players trained on the top deck of the ship. Jules Rimet (after whom the World Cup trophy was named) also travelled on the same ship with the World Cup trophy packed in his suitcase.
- The first FIFA World Cup in Uruguay was hosted in three stadiums, including the purpose-built Centenario in the capital of Uruguay, Montevideo. All the matches were played in one city: Montevideo.
- The stadium Estadio Centenario was built specifically to celebrate host Uruguay's 100th birthday, and it wasn't completed until the fifth day into the

tournament. It appears Uruguay was surprised to be given the rights to host the first World Cup.

- This was the first footballing event to introduce the round-robin concept in the group stage. Nine Olympic football tournaments had taken place before this without this innovative concept that exists to date.
- Strangely, there was no official ball for the tournament, and each team brought its own ball to play with. These leather balls were so hard and heavy that the Bolivian players played with berets.
- The first World Cup match took place on 13 July 1930 between France and Mexico. The venue was Montevideo, and France won the match 4–1.
- French footballer Lucien Laurent has only scored 2 goals for his country. But he will be remembered in history as the scorer of the first World Cup goal against Mexico in the 19th minute of the match. That's a great story for the grandkids.
- During the Peru versus Romania game in the 1930 World Cup, Peru's Plácido Galindo became the first-ever player in the history of the World Cup to be sent off over a red card after 70 minutes of play.
- However, the Peru versus Romania game was not so exciting in terms of viewership as only 300 people turned up to watch the match at Estadio Pocitos in Montevideo on 14 July 1930. The final on 30 July 1930 at Estadio Centenario had 93,000 spectators in comparison.
- The team from Romania was selected by King Carol II of Romania himself. The players were promised jobs and cash rewards after the tournament.

- The USA and Romania employed even more creative strategies in their team selection. When Scotland refused to play in the World Cup, these two countries simply hired the Scottish players who played for the USA and Romania. One world!
- The youngest coach for a World Cup football team was Juan José Tramutola. He was only 27 years and 267 days old when Argentina played France in the 1930 World Cup. Chile's coach György Orth was 29 years old.
- The first player to be expelled from the World Cup was Uruguay's goalkeeper Andrés Mazali. He was banned forever from the national team when he sneaked out of the team hotel, an act prohibited by strict Uruguayan trainer Alberto Suppici.
- The Yugoslavian football team for the inaugural World Cup in 1930 had the youngest starting line-up ever. The average age of the players in the team was 21 years and 258 months. They knocked out Brazil in their first-ever World Cup game 2–1.
- Bolivia's football team wore shirts which together spelt VIVA URUGUAY. This was a united Bolivian effort to salute their neighbours, Uruguay, for receiving the honour of hosting the first football World Cup.
- In a rematch of the gold medal match of the 1928 Olympics, Argentina and hosts Uruguay met in the final of the inaugural World Cup. 68,346 people watched this match, which Uruguay won 4–2. The winning goal was scored by Uruguayan Héctor Castro, who had just one arm.

- The football associations of South American neighbours Argentina and Uruguay used different footballs. The Argentine ball was lighter, while the Uruguayan ball was heavier. There was a heated argument between the two countries as to which ball should be used in the 1930 World Cup final.
- When neither Argentina nor Uruguay refused to budge from their stance of using their own footballs in the final, the Belgian referee Jean Langenus came up with a solution. He used the lighter Argentine ball in the first half and the heavier Uruguayan ball in the second half.
- Guillermo Stábile scored in the 37th minute to give Argentina a 2–1 lead in the 1930 World Cup final. Uruguay won a famous victory as they came from behind to win 4–2. Guillermo Stábile was the top scorer of the 1930 World Cup, scoring 8 goals throughout the tournament.
- The first final of the first World Cup was full of tension as both sides wanted to win rather badly. In the final, 300 soldiers were deployed in the stadium during the match between Argentina and Uruguay to cool down the tension between the fans.
- 15,000 Argentine supporters set off on a ship to join the thousands already there to watch the World Cup final. But this ship got lost at sea because of heavy fog and reached Montevideo only a day after the final. When the fans heard that Argentina had lost the final, they began riots in Uruguay's capital.
- The Argentinian players were also the bad boys in the World Cup. Police were called to control the violence

Portrait Sketch of Alexandre Villaplane

during their 6–1 win over Chile. In the semi-final against the USA, an Argentinian tackle caused a broken leg that caused a mass brawl. An Argentine player uprooted four teeth of an American while another ended up in hospital with injuries.

- In 1944, Alexandre Villaplane, the captain of the French team in 1930, was executed for collaborating with the Germans during World War II.
- The last surviving player of the 1930 World Cup was Argentina's Francisco Varallo. He passed away on 30

August 2010 after the World Cup in South Africa at the age of 100.

- Romanian footballer Alfred Feraru fell ill during the trip back home. On a stopover in Italy's Genoa, he was hospitalized as the ship left for Romania. A rumour broke out later that Feraru had died. His mother started making funeral arrangements and fainted in shock when Feraru returned a healthy man.
- Francisco Matteucci of Uruguay became the youngest referee to officiate in a World Cup game when he was put in charge of the match between Yugoslavia and Bolivia.

1934 World Cup Facts

- In the second World Cup in 1934, even the host nation Italy had to qualify for the finals and did not receive an automatic berth. Italy easily beat Greece in the qualifiers and went on to win the first of their four World Cup titles.
- Swedish referee Ivan Eklind became the youngest-ever referee to officiate in 2 successive World Cup tournaments. In the 1934 edition, he was only 28 years old, and he was 32 years old at the 1938 World Cup.
- 27 May 1934 witnessed the first extra-time match in World Cup history. Austria emerged victorious over France in a Round of 16 knockout match, winning 3–2 after extra time.
- 32 teams appeared for the qualifying rounds for the main tournament. Out of this, only 16 teams were chosen to play in the 1934 FIFA World Cup. The

Italian government allocated 3.5 million lire for the event.

- Uruguay, the winners of the inaugural World Cup in 1930 and title defenders, refused to participate in the 1934 World Cup. This was because only four European nations had accepted their invitation to play in the 1930 World Cup.
- The 1934 World Cup is the only one in history where all 8 quarter-finalists were from Europe. A total of 70 goals were scored in the tournament, with Czechoslovakia's Oldřich Nejedlý becoming the top scorer with 5 goals.
- Many media outlets reported that the Italian dictator Benito Mussolini influenced the tournament somewhat by assigning referees of his choice for the Italian team games. Bribery and corruption charges were also alleged during the tournament that Italy won.

1938 World Cup Facts

- The 1938 World Cup was held in France with the threat of war hovering over Europe. 37 teams participated in the qualifying rounds with 16 teams making it to the main round. 13 of the teams were from Europe, and Brazil was the only South American team in the tournament.
- The tournament saw the addition of 30 minutes of extra time if the two teams were tied after 90 minutes of regular time. In case the match was still tied, a rematch was scheduled the next day. The penalty

shoot-out hadn't been invented then. 6 games went into extra time.

- Polish striker Ernest Wilimowski struck 4 goals against Brazil, becoming the first player to do so in a World Cup. But even this superlative feat was not a match-winning performance against Brazil. Leônidas scored a hat-trick in Brazil's 6–5 win over Poland after the match ended 4–4 in normal time.
- The Dutch East Indies (Indonesia) arrived to play the 1938 World Cup without having to play in the qualifying rounds as they were the first country to represent the Asian Confederation. They are the only country to play just 1 match in the World Cup as they were eliminated after being humiliated 6–0 by Hungary.
- Italy beat Brazil in the semi-finals thanks to Giuseppe Meazza's rather unusual penalty. As he lined up to take the kick, his shorts fell. The Italian still managed to beat the laughing Brazilian goalkeeper despite this short handicap taking Italy to the final. He who laughs last…
- Although Brazil exited in the semi-finals, its players made an impact, winning many fans. Leônidas da Silva was the star Brazilian player, famous for his speed and for being one of the pioneers of the bicycle kick.
- The FIFA World Cup could not be held for 12 long years because of World War II. So, Italy, the world champions in both 1934 and 1938, were the reigning World Cup holders for a record 16 years, from 1934 to 1950.

- Dr Ottorino Barassi, the Italian vice president of FIFA, was determined not to let the FIFA World Cup trophy be seized by the Nazi troops. He hid it under his bed through the course of World War II, producing it again before the 1950 World Cup.
- The only manager to win the FIFA World Cup twice was Italian manager Vittorio Pozzo. Under him, Italy won in 1934, as well as in 1938. Pozzo was 52 years old during the second World Cup triumph by the Italians in 1938.

1950 World Cup Facts

- The oldest footballer at the 1950 World Cup was Englishman Stanley Matthews, who was 35 years old. Surprisingly, Matthews did not hang up his boots after the 1950 World Cup as expected but carried on, representing England for seven more years, retiring only in 1965.
- Yugoslavia's coach in 1950, Milorad Arsenijević was a World Cup veteran, also having represented his country in the 1930 World Cup as a player. He was the first man to appear in the World Cup in both roles – as a player and a coach.
- History was created in the 1950 FIFA World Cup as the defending champions Italy were defeated in the very first round by Sweden. This shock defeat was the first for any defending champion in the tournament's history.
- Another major upset that happened in the 1950 World Cup was when Joe Gaetjens scored in the 38th minute

for the USA against England in the first round. The Americans won the match 1–0.

- The 1950 World Cup also saw the largest attendance of a World Cup match till then. 1,99,854 people turned up at the stadium to watch the match between Brazil and Uruguay in Rio de Janeiro in July 1950.
- The traditional format of a final match was broken by FIFA in the 1950 World Cup. Instead of a final match after the knockout stages, the tournament was divided into four groups, the winners of which advanced to a final group.
- India's national football team qualified for the 1950 tournament but withdrew because of financial concerns like travelling to the venue. It also could not meet FIFA's requirement for players to wear shoes during matches since the Indian players only played barefoot.
- The final group had four teams with Brazil and Uruguay making it to the Top 2 on points, with Brazil the favourites to win the Cup. So, the group match between Brazil and Uruguay determined the champion. Despite being the favourites, Brazil lost 2–1, and Uruguay became the champions without playing a final.
- 23 year-old Uruguay player Alcides Ghiggia scored the winning goal against Brazil in the final at Rio's Maracanã Stadium. Later, Ghiggia famously said, 'Only three people have ever silenced 200,000 people at the Maracanã with a single gesture: Frank Sinatra, Pope John Paul II and me.'
- The oldest referee to officiate in a World Cup game was George Reader of England. Reader was 53 years

Commemorative Stamp featuring Alcides Ghiggia

old when he was the referee of the World Cup final in 1950 between Brazil and Uruguay. Old boy George certainly Read the game well!

1954 World Cup Facts

- The 1954 FIFA World Cup hosted in Switzerland was historic as it involved the first live television transmission of the event. This led to the fuelling of worldwide interest in both football and the FIFA World Cup.
- South Korean goalkeeper Hong Deok-young went down in football history for the wrong reason. He

became the goalkeeper to concede the most goals in a World Cup. In 1954, he conceded as many as 16 goals.

- The team manager of France, Gaston Barreau, was 70 years and 194 days old when France faced Mexico in the 1954 World Cup.
- The 1954 World Cup also saw the use of shirt numbers or jersey numbers for the very first time. The jersey numbers that have produced the maximum goals from then to the present are 9, 10, 11, 8, and 7.
- The 1954 World Cup saw many high-scoring thrillers like Austria's 7–5 win over Switzerland in Lausanne, which was the highest-scoring game in World Cup history then, and Hungary's 8–3 win over West Germany in Basle.
- West German coach Sepp Herberger played a reserve West German team in the group-stage match against Hungary and lost 8–3. Puskás & Co. of Hungary were in raging form in 1954 having thrashed debutants Korea Republic 9–0. So, one needed something special to beat them.
- Coach Sepp Herberger's strategy ensured that West Germany won its first World Cup title in 1954. When West Germany faced Hungary again in the final, Herberger started with his best team, which took the fancied Hungarians by surprise. West Germany won 3–2, and this is known as the 'Miracle of Bern'.
- Hungary entered the World Cup as firm favourites as they were undefeated in their previous 28 games in international football with 24 wins and four draws.

Their undefeated streak was broken by West Germany in the final.

- In 1954, Hungary also scored the most goals by one team in a single tournament. They scored a total of 27 goals in Switzerland.

1958 World Cup Facts

- The 1958 World Cup in Sweden was revolutionary, being the first World Cup that received international television coverage. For the first time, people from all over the world saw their favourite footballers on television compete to win football's most prestigious event.
- Incidentally, Scotland has qualified for the World Cup as many as eight times. But it has always failed to advance beyond the first round of the competition. That's a record they will look to improve if they manage to qualify again.
- Speaking of first-round exits, Argentina suffered the same in 1958. The team was greeted with garbage thrown by angry Argentinian fans at the airport when they landed back in Buenos Aires.
- The legendary Argentinian player Alfredo di Stéfano got Spanish citizenship. In 1957, he played four World Cup qualifying matches for Spain, but sadly, Spain failed to qualify for the 1958 World Cup. Alfredo Di Stéfano is regarded as the greatest player never to have played in the World Cup.
- The highest-scoring game in this World Cup was when France beat Paraguay 7–3. The centre forward Just

Fontaine was the French star of the tournament and was only eclipsed by Pelé. Remarkably, the highest scorer of the tournament was not even a part of France's initial first team.

- The Morocco-born Just Fontaine found a place in the French starting line-up only after first-choice French player René Bliard hurt his ankle in training before the tournament began. He was forced to return home, and Fontaine took his place to run riot, creating a record yet to be broken.
- However, the quarter-finals of the 1958 World Cup were a bit of a dampener as none of the four losing teams could score a single goal during these knockout games.
- Pelé also scored a hat-trick of records. He became the youngest player to score a goal at the World Cup at 17 years and 239 days, scoring against Wales in the quarter-finals. He became the youngest player to win the World Cup and is also the only player to win three World Cups (1958, 1962, and 1970) till date.
- The match of the tournament was the semi-finals between Brazil and France. Although Brazil won 5–2, it was almost even at half-time with Brazil hanging on to a slender lead of 2–1. Then, Pelé scored a hat-trick in 20 minutes in the second half to seal the victory.
- Pelé is also part of an exclusive footballing club of three members. They have all scored goals in four World Cups. Pelé for Brazil (1958–70), Uwe Seeler for West Germany (1958–70), and Miroslav Klose for Germany (2002–14).

- The 1958 FIFA World Cup saw the highest number of goals scored in a final. 7 goals were scored! The final was played in Stockholm on Sunday, 29 June 1958 with Brazil facing Sweden. Brazil defeated Sweden 5–2 to lift the Cup and create an unbroken record.
- The innovative 4–2–4 formation was introduced by Brazil in the 1958 World Cup. This formation was totally different from the traditional pyramid formation (2–3–5) and other formations employed during the time. The successful implementation of this formation was a key element of Brazil's success.
- Brazil's 4–2–4 formation had two centre forwards who were supported by two wingers when they attacked. By their forceful attacking play, Brazil forced their opponents to go on the defensive as eight Brazilians

The 4-2-4 Formation

were attacking instead of six. Many teams switched to this formation after the World Cup.

- The 1958 World Cup was the only World Cup when all four teams from Great Britain – England, Scotland, Wales, and Northern Ireland – managed to qualify for the same tournament. England had an impressive game against Brazil in the first round in a goalless draw, which was the first-ever goalless game at the World Cup.

1962 World Cup Facts

- The Great Chile Earthquake in 1960 devastated the country. It was the most powerful quake in history, recorded as 9.5 on the Richter scale. Hence, it was a big challenge for the South American nation to host an event of the magnitude of the World Cup in 1962.
- The Chileans were angry because of Italian newspaper reports that criticized the standard of living in Chile just before their first-round match in the 1962 World Cup. The game was a rough one with violence on the pitch resulting in two players receiving red cards and two fracture injuries. This match was named 'The Battle of Santiago'.
- The Chileans displayed great character to rebuild the nation to host the World Cup successfully after two years. The Chile football team also displayed great courage and skill on the pitch as they upset footballing giants like Italy and the USSR to reach the semi-finals of the tournament and secure a third-place finish.

- For the first time in the history of the World Cup, there was no tinkering in the earlier format as FIFA somehow resisted the temptation to do so. The rules were the same as the 1958 World Cup.
- Pelé is the only footballer in World Cup history to have won three World Cups (1958, 1962 and 1970). But Pelé missed a major portion of the 1962 edition, going out in the second round because of injury. Brazil was still strong enough to lift the Cup thanks to other iconic players like Garrincha.
- The European teams adopted the defensive 'catenaccio' style of play popularized then by Italian club Inter Milan. This was what resulted in the extreme foul play and putting Pelé out of action. But it also proved that ultra-defensive tactics were not enough to win a World Cup.
- The Brazilian team faced a shocker when Garrincha was sent off in the semi-finals. In a bizarre turn of events, Brazilian prime minister Tancredo Neves managed to get Garrincha's ban overturned by FIFA. Garrincha was the star of the 1962 World Cup and was the joint top-scorer of the tournament.
- The 1962 World Cup was unique as six players, including Brazil's Garrincha, scored 4 goals each and finished tied as the tournament's top scorers. This speaks volumes about the sheer goal-scoring talent on offer in 1962 even with the great Pelé injured.
- Brazil and Czechoslovakia faced each other in the final, the latter reaching the finals thanks to the heroics of their outstanding goalkeeper Jilhelm Schroiff. Ironically, it was Schroiff's blunders that gave Brazil

a 3–1 victory and their second successive World Cup triumph. Brazilian Vavá became the first player to score in consecutive finals.

- Pelé had to wait 45 years to receive the World Cup medal Brazil won in 1962. As Pelé was injured in the second round, he missed the tournament and the gold medal after that. Astonishingly, FIFA realized this mistake only in 2017 and gave Pelé the gold medal he deserved. Well, stranger things have happened in football.

1966 World Cup Facts

- Just four months before the 1966 World Cup, thieves stole the Jules Rimet Trophy from an exhibition at the Westminster Central Hall. The trophy was discovered by a little dog named Pickles under a bush. The owner of Pickles was given a reward of 6,000 British pounds.
- An entire continent boycotted the 1966 World Cup because of a FIFA ruling that only one team would be allowed to compete from the Afro-Asian countries. Thirty-one African teams boycotted the Cup in England as a protest against the unfair ruling.
- The FIFA ruling that was objectionable to the Africans stated that the three second-round winners from the African zone had to play against the winners of the Asian zone to qualify. The African nations felt that winning their zone was enough to qualify for the World Cup.
- Greyhound racing was more popular in England than football in 1966. Hosts England were scheduled to

play all their games at Wembley. But after a conflict of dates with the regular Greyhound Meeting, an England World Cup game had to be moved and rescheduled.

- No wonder tickets for the 1966 final were available for as little as 10 shillings. That's around 50p in today's money, or US$11, adjusting for inflation. But football has become the predominant sport after England won the World Cup in 1966.
- Portugal striker Eusébio shone for Portugal in 1966 as did Geoff Hurst for England. Eusébio scored 4 goals in a remarkable comeback for Portugal against Korea DPR while Geoff Hurst scored a hat-trick in the final against West Germany. But one of the goals is the most controversial in World Cup history.
- Portugal appeared to be shocked as North Korea took a 3–0 lead after just 22 minutes into the game in the quarter-finals. But North Korean dreams of playing the semi-final were dashed by Eusébio and company as the Portuguese stormed back to win the game 5–3.
- England ended Portugal's fine run in the semi-finals of the 1966 World Cup. Although a heavily marked Eusébio scored a late goal for Portugal with a penalty, Bobby Charlton scored a fine brace as England won 2–1 to enter the final.
- Russian goalkeeper Lev Yashin is considered the greatest goalkeeper ever by many football experts. He played in three World Cups from 1958 to 1966 and was nicknamed 'Black Spider' for his all-black goalkeeper attire. He made as many as 63 saves in his World Cup appearances.

Lev Yashin

- When the great Lev Yashin was asked how he prepared before a match, he famously replied, 'I like to have a smoke before a match to calm my nerves, then drink a strong drink to tone my muscles.'

1970 World Cup Facts

- The World Cup reached North America for the first time when Mexico hosted it for the first time in 1970. 16 teams from all six continents participated in the 1970 FIFA World Cup. Brazil were the winners, defeating Italy 4–1 in the final.

- The official FIFA World Cup match balls that we see today were first launched in this tournament. The first ball, Adidas Telstar, had 32 black-and-white panels. It was more visible on black-and-white televisions, and this was the first World Cup that was broadcast live on television worldwide in colour.
- Yellow cards and substations were first implemented in the 1970 World Cup. The first player to be cautioned with the first yellow card was the USSR's Kakhi Asatiani. Chilean player Carlos Caszely received the first red card.
- Substitutions were first made during the 1970 World Cup. Each team was allowed to make two substitutions every game for the first time in World Cup history.
- Although Peru couldn't perform as well as Brazil, the Peruvian players grabbed eyeballs in their classic white jerseys featuring a bright-red diagonal slash from shoulder to waist.
- The semi-final between Italy and West Germany at the Azteca Stadium was termed as the 'Game of the Century'. The match saw 7 goals with 5 goals happening in the 30 minutes of extra time that was brought about by a last-minute West German equalizer.
- For the first time in the history of the FIFA World Cup, all four semi-finalists were previous Cup winners. The teams were Uruguay, Brazil, Italy, and Germany. This has been repeated just once later, in Italia 1990.
- Brazil became the first team to win the coveted trophy for the third time, thus earning the Jules Rimet Trophy

forever as a new golden trophy was introduced after this World Cup.

- This edition of the World Cup was famous for its high-scoring games. A total of 95 goals were scored in 32 matches. That's an average of almost 3 goals per game.
- Pelé was the star of the 1970 World Cup. He scored 4 goals and set up 6 assists to help Brazil lift the Cup. He was named the Player of the Tournament.
- The most memorable match was the semi-final between West Germany and Italy, hailed by many critics as the greatest match in World Cup history. Germany's Karl-Heinz Schnellinger scored in the 90th minute to tie the score 1–1, sending the game into extra time. The Italians snatched a dramatic 4–3 extra-time win.
- The Jules Rimet Trophy that was stolen and recovered in 1966 was stolen again in 1983. But this time, it was never found. Brazil was awarded the trophy permanently after their 1970 win as the FIFA World Cup trophy replaced this one. The Brazilian Football Confederation has been given a replica.
- Before kick-off in a game, as Pelé was tying his boot laces, the cameras zoomed in to reveal the Brazilian striker's Puma boots. After that, Puma boots sold like hot cakes thanks to Pelé.
- Italian defender Tarcisio Burgnich was assigned the tough responsibility of marking Pelé in the 1970 World Cup final. He said later, 'I told myself before the game, he's made of skin and bones just like everyone else – but I was wrong.'

Mário Zagallo

- Mário Zagallo became the first man to win the World Cup both as a player and a coach. He won the World Cup as a player for Brazil in 1958 and 1962. He won the World Cup as a manager in 1970 as well as an assistant manager in 1994. That's some feat!
- The trophy awarded to the best goalkeeper in the World Cup is named after Lev Yashin. Despite his performance, the best the Russians could manage was fourth place in 1966. But it's ironic that the man after whom the best goalkeeper trophy is named was a substitute in 1970 at the age of 41.
- Almost 90 million people around the world watched the 1970 World Cup final on television, making it one of the most-watched sporting events of all time then.

1974 World Cup Facts

- The 1974 FIFA World Cup was hosted by West Germany from 13 June to 7 July and was the tenth edition of the popular tournament. A new trophy was introduced in this tournament called the FIFA World Cup trophy, which replaced the earlier Jules Rimet Trophy.
- The official mascots of the 1974 World Cup were two boys named Tip and Tap, dressed in soccer uniforms of West Germany. Similar to 1970's Telstar, Telstar Durlast was the official ball of the 1974 World Cup.
- The 1974 World Cup had 16 teams competing for top honours. In the group stage, each team played 3 matches, and the top two teams from each group advanced to the second round. Surprisingly, Brazil failed to qualify for this World Cup.
- The goal difference rule was first implemented in the 1974 World Cup to choose the winner of a group if two teams finished with the same points. Earlier, a play-off match decided the winner of a group.
- Many African teams, like Zaire (now known as the Democratic Republic of Congo) and Haiti, made their World Cup debuts in 1974. Sadly, Haitian defender Ernst Jean-Joseph was the first man to fail a doping test at the World Cup.
- The Zaire goalkeeper was replaced when his team was losing 0–3 after 22 minutes to Yugoslavia. This was the first time in the World Cup that a goalkeeper was replaced for performance rather than injury. Sadly, his

replacement Dimbi Tubilandu let in 6 more goals for Zaire to lose 9–0.

- We also saw the first penalty shoot-out in the knockout stages in this World Cup when West Germany beat Poland in the quarter-finals after a goalless draw. Five players from West Germany won gold, silver, and bronze medals, which was a first at that point of time.
- Famous West Indian cricketer Sir Viv Richards is the only man to have participated in both World

Sir Vivian Richards

Cup cricket and World Cup football. He also played football for Antigua in the 1974 World Cup qualifiers.

- Polish player Lesław Ćmikiewicz set a new record in this World Cup when he appeared as a substitute as many as six times. Ćmikiewicz went on to become a successful manager, too.
- Gerd Müller of West Germany was the top scorer of the tournament with 4 goals. He also scored the winner against the Netherlands in the final. But the tournament saw many stars like Johan Cruyff (Netherlands), Franz Beckenbauer (West Germany), and Kazimierz Deyna (Poland).
- Dutch legend Johan Cruyff demonstrated his famous 'Cruyff turn' in 1974 for the first time when he fooled Swedish defender Jan Olsson to go past him.
- The 'Total Football' style was introduced by the Netherlands under their mercurial captain Johan Cruyff. This extremely fluid style of play had everyone behind the ball and any player could play in any position, except the goalkeeper.

Total Football, Johan Cruyff and the Dutch Team of the 1970s

- But despite impressing everyone with their style, the Dutch lost in the final to West Germany 2–1. This was West Germany's second World Cup triumph, the first coming in 1954. If it was any consolation for the Dutch, Cruyff was the top scorer of the tournament and also won the award for Best Player.

1978 World Cup Facts

- The 1978 FIFA World Cup was held in Argentina in June and was the 11th edition of the international soccer tournament. There were 16 teams divided into four groups. The top two teams from each group would move to another group stage, and the winner of each group would play the final.
- More than 100 countries watched this World Cup on television, and almost 1.5 billion people watched the final. A new ball, the Adidas Tango, was introduced with a new design and a more accurate flight path.
- The official mascot of the 1978 World Cup was a boy named Gauchito with a football. He wore an Argentina jersey with 'Argentina 78' on his hat and also sported a neckerchief and a whip that were typical of a gaucho, the cowboy of the South American Pampas.
- The French team arrived for the World Cup without an alternate jersey. Problems arose in their first-round match against Hungary as both teams' jerseys were white. The French had to borrow jerseys from a local team named Atlético Kimberley, who played 2 km away from the Mar del Plata Stadium.

- The jersey that the French team borrowed from Atlético Kimberley and played in was rather unique in design. These green-and-white striped jerseys made their first and last appearance in a World Cup as the French played in them. It was quite a sight!
- Berti Vogts scored a famous own goal against Austria in Cordoba in 1978 in his 96th and final international match. It didn't end as well as Vogts had hoped since West Germany lost 3–2 to their neighbours, Austria, for the first time in almost 50 years.
- 17-year-old Diego Maradona did not make it into the 1978 World Cup team as coach César Luis Menotti believed he was too young then. Opinion is still divided as to whether this was the right decision by Menotti.
- Argentina's star of the tournament was Mario Kempes, who scored 6 goals to become the top scorer. But Peru also pulled off a remarkable feat to reach the semi-finals. The only South Americans to do so previously were Uruguay, Brazil, and Argentina.
- Peru's fantastic run was ended by Argentina in the semi-finals. However, Argentina needed to win by 4 goals to reach the finals of the tournament, which seemed to be an impossible task the way Peru was playing. To everyone's surprise, Argentina won 6–0, which intensified the allegations of match-fixing.
- The Peru versus Argentina semi-final in Buenos Aires was also tragic apart from being controversial. A stampede in the stadium killed 55 spectators. Crowd management was a problem as over 1.5 million people watched the games with an average of 40,000 spectators per game.

- There were quite a few other upsets in the tournament as the African team Tunisia beat Mexico 3–1 and the Asian team Iran shocked Scotland 1–0. Hungary beat eventual champions Argentina 3–1 in the second group stage.
- The tournament was full of controversy as Argentina's military government was accused of using the World Cup as a propaganda tool to divert the people from the country's political problems. Well, it certainly paid off as Argentina won its first-ever World Cup, beating the Dutch 3–1 in the final.
- Other controversial elements that were alleged were political interference in the team selection of Argentina and widespread reports of match-fixing in the games. But no Argentinian was complaining after the Cup.

1982 World Cup Facts

- For the first time in the history of the FIFA World Cup, it was hosted in Southern Europe. Spain hosted the 1982 World Cup where 24 teams took part for the first time, a jump up from the previous 16 teams.
- A new ball named the Adidas Tango España was designed specifically for the 1982 World Cup. It had a new design with 20 white hexagons and 12 black pentagons.
- The 1982 World Cup was special as it had some of the greatest footballers in the world competing against each other, like Zico, Diego Maradona, Michel Platini, and Paolo Rossi. The Italian striker Paolo Rossi won

Paolo Rossi's Bronze Statue, World Cup champion of the 1982 FIFA World Cup in Spain

top honours by winning the Golden Boot for 6 goals scored in the tournament.

- Spain's Emilio Butragueño was another special player in 1982. His playing style was termed 'Vulture Culture'. The Vulture scored 4 goals in the quarter-final against Denmark, helping hosts Spain reach the semi-finals for the first time in their football history.

- But the most special match in the 1982 World Cup was probably the second-round showdown between Italy and Brazil. Paolo Rossi scored an electrifying hat-trick, helping Italy win the contest 3–2 and knocking Brazil out of the World Cup.
- One semi-final saw another thriller as West Germany beat France 5–4 in a penalty shoot-out after the match was drawn 3–3 after extra time. But West Germany lost 3–1 to Italy in the final, where Paolo Rossi scored a brace.
- Dino Zoff, captain of the Italian team in 1982, was the oldest player to win the World Cup finals at 40 years, four months and 13 days. Northern Ireland's Norman Whiteside became the youngest player to play in the FIFA World Cup. He was only 17 years and 41 days old when he played against Yugoslavia in 1982.
- The only substitute to score a hat-trick in the World Cup was Hungary's László Kiss. He scored the first 3 goals for Hungary in just 7 minutes against El Salvador in 1982.
- Spain hosted the 1982 World Cup for the first and only time to date. Sadly, their performance was the worst ever by a host nation (matched by Qatar at the 2022 World Cup) as they won 1 in 5 matches and exited in the first round, placed bottom of their group.
- The 1982 semi-final between France and Germany was a spectacular match. An injured Karl-Heinz Rummenigge entered the pitch as a substitute in the dying minutes of the match. He scored 2 goals, the second in the penalty shoot-out to ensure the dramatically famous German come-from-behind victory.

- László Kiss came on as a substitute for Hungary in the 77th minute of the match against Salvador to score 3 goals in quick time. Kiss earned the distinction of becoming the only substitute in World Cup history to record a hat-trick.
- In 1982, legendary Polish footballer Zbigniew Boniek became the 36th player to score a hat-trick in the World Cup. He pumped 3 goals into the Belgian net. Boniek was one of the best players in his era and was sadly suspended for the semi-finals against Italy. Poland lost 2–0 in Boniek's absence.

1986 World Cup Facts

- Mexico hosted the 1986 FIFA World Cup, and this was the second time the country hosted the World Cup, the first being in 1970. 24 teams participated in the event watched by almost 2.3 billion people across the world.
- The format was changed in the 1986 World Cup, and a knockout system prevailed from the Round of 16, and this rule remains to date.
- Rafael Márquez of Mexico became the youngest player to play in a World Cup match at 17 years and 97 days.
- The tournament featured great footballers like Gary Lineker of England, Emilio Butragueño of Spain, Preben Elkjær Larsen of Denmark, and Enzo Francescoli of Uruguay. But the greatest of them all was Diego Maradona of Argentina.
- Maradona was the star of '86, scoring 5 goals and providing 5 assists in the tournament. His controversial

'Hand of God' goal, where he punched the ball into the goal with his left hand beating English goalkeeper Peter Shilton in mid-air, went undetected by the referee.

- Argentina beat England 2–1 in the quarter-finals, where Maradona scored both goals. The second goal was a masterpiece as Diego Maradona scored it after dribbling past five English players.
- Scottish fan group the 'Tartan Army' has a chant in praise of Diego Maradona for sending their neighbours England out of the 1986 World Cup. With a neighbour like that, who needs enemies?
- José Batista of Uruguay carved his name in the record books when he received a red card in only the 56th second of the first-round match against Scotland. This was the fastest ejection of a player in World Cup history.
- In the 1986 World Cup, FIFA banned shirt swapping between the players only because they did not want the footballers to bare their chests on the field.
- The 'Fair Play' award was first introduced in this tournament and was won by Brazil. The other South American nations like Uruguay did not believe much in fair play.
- The final of the 1986 World Cup was another classic as Karl Heinz Rummenigge's West Germany came from behind to make it 2–2 against Argentina. But Argentina scored a third to make it 3–2 and lifted the trophy for the second time.
- Marcelo Trobbiani was a substitute during Argentina's entire 1986 FIFA World Cup campaign. Surprisingly,

the coach brought him to play only in the final as a substitute during the last few seconds of the game. This was Argentina's only substitution in the 89th minute of the final against West Germany.

1990 World Cup Facts

- Italy hosted the 1990 FIFA World Cup, which was the 14th edition of the tournament. The official ball of this World Cup was the Adidas Etrusco Unico, named after the Etruscan civilization of ancient Italy.
- Cameroon were the dark horse and surprise package of Italia 90 as they shocked defending champions Argentina 1–0 in their opening encounter and reached the quarter-finals in their first-ever World Cup appearance. However, a Maradona-led Argentina still managed to reach the finals.
- 38-year-old Roger Milla from Cameroon was the oldest player to participate in this World Cup. The striker came on as a late substitute and became famous both for his goals and his unique celebrations by dancing around the corner flag after scoring.
- Despite losing to Cameroon in their opening match and Maradona receiving a red card in their second-round match against arch-rivals Brazil, Argentina reached the finals. But their luck ran out as they lost to West Germany 1–0. West Germany lifted the World Cup for the third time.
- Pedro Monzón of Argentina was the first player to be expelled in a World Cup final when he was sent off

Roger Milla

against West Germany in the 65th minute as Argentina were reduced to ten men.

- The player to have played the maximum World Cup matches was German captain and legend Lothar Matthäus. He played 25 games in five World Cups from 1982 to 1998. He was captain in two World Cups, including the victorious Italia 90.
- Although Lothar Matthäus has played the maximum number of World Cup matches, he shares the record for the maximum World Cups played with two Mexican footballers. Goalkeeper Antonio Carbajal played in five World Cups from 1950 to 1966 and Mexican Rafael Márquez captained his team in five World Cups from 2002 to 2018.

- Italia 90 saw a total of 115 goals scored in the tournament, and strangely, this was the lowest number of goals scored in a World Cup since 1978. It appears that the host team had infected everyone else with their excessive defensive play.
- Although England went down to Germany, English striker Gary Lineker proved his mettle, scoring 6 goals in Italia 90 and winning the Golden Boot award. But World Cup pressure got to Lineker as well as he pooped his pants in the game against Ireland.
- English hopes were dashed in the 99th minute in the 1990 semi-finals when they were reduced to ten men. English star player Paul Gascoigne was given a second yellow card, and he reacted with tears as he walked off the pitch.
- Italia 90 saw the impressive debut of the Republic of Ireland in the World Cup. The Republic of Ireland reached the quarter-finals in their very first World Cup appearance.
- The first-ever clean sheet in a FIFA World Cup final was kept by Bodo Illgner of West Germany who did not concede a goal in the final against Argentina. But Italian goalie Walter Zenga holds the record for not conceding a goal for 517 minutes in Italia 90.
- Italian goalie Walter Zenga's unbeaten streak in this World Cup was finally broken by Argentinian striker Claudio Caniggia when he scored in the 67th minute against Italy in the semi-finals.
- Robert Prosinečki has a unique record in World Cups as the only footballer ever to score a goal for two

different countries. In 1990, he scored for Yugoslavia against the UAE. Eight years later, he scored 2 goals for Croatia in 1998, who finished third in the tournament.

- Franz Beckenbauer became the second man in football history to win the World Cup title as a player as well as a coach. The Kaiser helped West Germany lift the World Cup as a key player in 1974. 16 years later, Beckenbauer won the title as the coach of the German national football team in 1990.

1994 World Cup Facts

- The 1994 World Cup hosted by the United States of America was the first World Cup to be held in North America. But it was a South American team that conquered North America as Brazil won a record fourth World Cup title.
- The tournament took place in nine American cities, including Los Angeles, New York, Washington, D.C. and Dallas. A total attendance of 35,87,538 was observed in the stadiums, averaging 68,991 spectators per match. This was a record attendance for a World Cup tournament then.
- During the opening ceremony, American singer Diana Ross led an elaborate song-and-dance number that culminated with a grand salute. Then, Ross was supposed to kick the ball inside an open goal. In a comic moment, Ross missed the open net by a long shot. But the goal still tore open on cue.
- The mascot for the USA 1994 World Cup was a cartoon dog called Striker. Warner Bros. designed

Striker, Official Mascot of the FIFA World Cup 1994

Striker and gave him a red, white, and blue soccer uniform.

- The implementation of new technologies was first seen in USA 94, like the use of 'vanishing spray' to mark free-kick distances and the use of digital advertising boards.
- The US team made it to the Round of 16, which was their best performance since the 1930 World Cup.
- Cameroon failed to impress like the earlier World Cup as Russia thrashed them 6–1. Russian footballer Oleg Salenko set a record by scoring 5 goals in a single game at the World Cup.

- When 24-year-old Roger Milla was playing international football for Cameroon, Rigobert Song was born. In USA 94, the 42-year-old Roger Milla lined up to play alongside a 17-year-old Song. This was the largest age difference between two on-field teammates in a World Cup game. Presently, Song manages Cameroon.
- The first goalkeeper to be shown a red card and sent off during a World Cup was Italian goalkeeper Gianluca Pagliuca on 23 June 1994. In Italy's game against Norway, Pagliuca handled the ball outside the penalty box in the 21st minute.
- USA 94 was the first World Cup since 1938 when none of the four teams from the UK – England, Northern Ireland, Scotland, and Wales – could qualify for the FIFA World Cup.
- On 5 July 1994, 28-year-old Italian striker Gianfranco Zola received a birthday present from coach Arrigo Sacchi when he played his first World Cup game against Nigeria. But Zola became the only player to receive a red card on his birthday and was sent off after 12 minutes.
- Later, replays showed that Zola's tackle on Nigerian defender Augustine Eguavoen was a legitimate one and the referee had made a mistake. Zola had to sit out in the quarter-final and semi-final and was not picked for the final, which Italy lost on penalties. Zola's World Cup career lasted for only 12 minutes.
- Despite Zola's premature exit, the Italian team performed admirably. Roberto Baggio scored a goal in the 87th minute in the quarter-finals to send Spain crashing out of the World Cup.

- First in World Cup history, the final was the highest-scoring goalless draw. In the final played at the Rose Bowl in Pasadena, California, Brazil and Italy failed to score against each other even after extra time. Brazil won 3–2 on penalties.
- Russian Oleg Salenko received the Golden Boot at the 1994 World Cup having scored 6 goals. This is the first time that a player won the award playing for a team that exited in the group stage. Surprisingly, these 6 goals were the only ones Salenko ever scored in his international career.

1998 World Cup Facts

- 32 teams battled for the top footballing prize in the 16th edition of the FIFA World Cup in 1998 which was hosted by France for the first time from 10 June to 12 July.
- 2.7 million spectators thronged the stadiums, with an average attendance of over 43,000 per match.
- FIFA decided to reward the success of African football in the earlier editions and gave Africa a well-deserved five places in the 32-team 1998 World Cup finals.
- As the rooster is a symbol of France, the official mascot of the World Cup was a rooster named Footix. The official match ball was the Adidas Tricolore, the first football to avail of a new technology that made it more stable and predictable in flight.
- The tournament was not free of controversies and conspiracy theories. One of the major ones came in the

Footix, Official Mascot of the FIFA World Cup 1998

finals, when Ronaldo was replaced (with Edmundo) and then reinstated at a gap of one hour in the team sheets on the day of the match. At noon, he underwent a lengthy treatment on his knees and was to rest after that. However, the siesta period was disturbed when his roommate Roberto Carlos witnessed Ronaldo having convulsions. After receiving treatment, he fell asleep but woke up feeling groggy, and was taken to a clinic for examination. He left for stadium from the clinic in evening. Meanwhile, Zagallo was preparing the team for a match without Ronaldo. Suddenly, he received a phone call from Ricardo Teixeira, president of Brazilian Football Confederation (CBF), that Ronaldo was on his way back and that he should play. This sparked arguments among the players, enraged Edmundo that he would be dropped, and concerns among the medical staff regarding Ronaldo's health. Ultimately, Ronaldo played the final but was only a shadow of himself, with a total of twenty ball touches in his tally. Conspiracy theories, from team sponsors (mainly Nike) insisting (through Teixeira) that Ronaldo had to start, to secret agreements being made between the French and Brazilian governments, were rife. Some others were that convulsions were a side effect of the anti-inflammatory drug Voltaren, which Ronaldo took for his injury; that he was misdiagnosed and mistreated, etc. Whatever the real reason be, it costed Brazil the World Cup as they lost the match 0–3 to France.

- 1998 saw major footballing stars on the pitch, like Brazilians Ronaldo, Rivaldo, and Roberto Carlos, Frenchmen Zinedine Zidane and Thierry Henry, and David Beckham of England. It also saw some spectacular goals, like Michael Owen's goal against Argentina in the Round of 16 and Dennis Bergkamp's magnificent goal against Argentina in the quarter-finals.
- In a great quarter-final between the Netherlands and Argentina, Dennis Bergkamp sealed the game in the 89th minute by controlling a 50-yard pass in the air from Frank de Boer, sidestepping defender Roberto

The Cup of Life by Ricky Martin

Ayala and smashing the ball into the roof of the net past goalkeeper Carlos Roa.

- The first official song of a World Cup was introduced in the 1998 FIFA World Cup. 'The Cup of Life' by Ricky Martin was a worldwide super hit.
- In 1998, Italian player Alessandro Nesta became the fastest substitute when he was replaced by Giuseppe Bergomi after just 4 minutes in a match against Austria. Wonder what the coach was thinking in the first place?
- Germany's starting line-up versus Iran in 1998 was the oldest team ever to play at a World Cup. The average age was 31 years and 345 days. Belgium came a close second as their average age in the match against Mexico was 31 years and 304 days.
- The first Golden Goal was scored by Laurent Blanc as his French team beat Paraguay 1–0 in extra time on 28 June 1998.
- Pierre Issa of South Africa could not find a place to hide in shame as he scored 2 own goals in the final

15 minutes against France. He was spared the record of the first player to score 2 own goals in a World Cup as the second goal was later credited to Thierry Henry of France.

- France won their first-ever World Cup, beating Brazil comprehensively by 3 goals to nil at the Stade de France in Saint-Denis to usher in a new era in French football.
- Bora Milutinović, coach of the Nigerian football team in 1998, became the only man in the history of World Cup football to coach five different countries. So what if none of them won the World Cup.

2002 World Cup Facts

- The FIFA World Cup arrived in Asia in 2002 and was co-hosted by South Korea and Japan. This was the first World Cup to be hosted jointly by two countries. A cartoon figure named Ato was the official mascot of the tournament, wearing a red and blue soccer uniform.
- It took 72 years for the World Cup to arrive in Asia and be hosted by Asian countries after 1930 when the inaugural World Cup was hosted by Uruguay. It was certainly worth the lengthy wait.
- Australia set the record for the highest-scoring match and largest margin of victory in a World Cup qualifying match. They scored 31 goals against American Samoa, and two days earlier, the Aussies embarrassed Tonga 22–0. With 13 goals, Archie Thompson broke his previous record of 10 goals against American Samoa.

- African nation Senegal shocked defending champions France 1–0 in the opening match of the World Cup. 64 matches were played in this World Cup between 32 teams, and 161 goals were scored.
- Germany striker Miroslav Klose became the 47th player in history to score a hat-trick at the World Cup. But what was unique was that all the 3 goals he scored against Saudi Arabia were powerful headers.
- The World Cup match ball used in this tournament was the Adidas Fevernova. This ball was designed for more speed and precision than earlier footballs used in the World Cup.
- A group game between Cameroon and Germany turned ugly, and as many as 12 yellow cards and 2 red cards were flashed by the referee to restore order in the match.
- Five players have scored a goal and been sent off in the same game. The last player to achieve this unique feat in the World Cup was Brazilian legend Ronaldinho. He was given the marching orders 7 minutes after scoring what would be the winning goal against England.
- Co-hosts South Korea created history by reaching the semi-finals of the World Cup. They upset European powerhouses Italy and Spain in the knockout stages and lost to Germany in the semi-finals.
- German goalie Oliver Kahn became the first goalkeeper to be awarded the Golden Ball in World Cup history after being adjudged the best player of the tournament in 2002.
- Brazil were the champions in 2002 after beating Germany 2–0 in the final. They won all their 7 matches

in the Cup. The last time they had achieved this feat was in 1970 when they won all their 6 matches in the World Cup.

- Brazilian striker Ronaldo received the Golden Boot as the top scorer of the tournament. He scored 8 goals, including both goals in the final against Germany.
- In the match for the third-place playoff, Turkey scored the quickest goal ever in the World Cup against South Korea. Turkish legend Hakan Şükür scored in just 10.8 seconds to set up a great thriller. South Korea came back into the game, but Turkey won 3–2.

2006 World Cup Facts

- Germany hosted the World Cup for the first time in its 18th edition in 2006 from 9 June to 9 July. A new record was set for attendance at a World Cup, with over 3.3 million spectators in the stadiums. 32 teams played a total of 64 matches.
- The official mascot for the 2006 World Cup was a lion called Goleo VI, with a talking football named Pille. The official match ball was the Adidas +Teamgeist, which boasted a new design with 14 curved panels.
- 26.29 billion people across the world watched all the matches in 2006. Seven and a half billion people saw the final match – almost a ninth of the total population on Earth.
- When Argentine legend Diego Maradona was invited to attend the opening ceremony of the 2006 World Cup in Germany, he refused, famously saying, 'I'm not here to look at bloody Pelé walking around.'

Goleo VI, Official Mascot of the FIFA World Cup 2006

- The tournament was full of upsets as defending champions Brazil bowed out in the quarter-finals and Argentina failed to progress beyond the group stage. In the final, Italy triumphed over France in a penalty shoot-out at the Olympiastadion in Berlin.
- Germany's Miroslav Klose was the top scorer of the tournament with 5 goals and received the Golden Boot.
- Confusion reigned supreme when English referee Graham Poll booked Croatian player Josip Šimunić three times before sending him off. Šimunić should have actually been given marching orders after the second yellow, but Poll got confused.

- The favourite colour of Russian referee Valentin Ivanov must be yellow! That explains his 16 yellow cards (which tied a tournament record) and 4 red cards in the second-round match at the 2006 World Cup between the Netherlands and Portugal. This match is known as the Massacre of Nuremberg.
- The dark side of the tournament was when Zinedine Zidane headbutted Italian Marco Materazzi in the final. This resulted in Zidane's red card, Italy winning the World Cup, and Zidane's eventual retirement from professional football.
- The Italians realized that Zidane was unstoppable, and Materazzi provoked him by insulting the Frenchman's sister. Zidane charged at him with his head and knocked the Italian over. Later, Materazzi admitted to the planned insult. That's why they say – always keep a cool head!
- The weirdest World Cup fact is that the birth rates go up in countries performing well in the World Cup because of general excitement and alcohol consumption. In 2006, when Germany hosted the tournament and was placed third, the birth rate in the country jumped by 10 per cent nine months later!

2010 World Cup Facts

- The 2010 FIFA World Cup was the first time the tournament was played in the continent of Africa. South Africa was the proud host. In another first, Spain became champions of the world for the first time after the title had eluded them for so many years.

- Nelson Mandela played a vital role in bringing the World Cup to the African continent for the first time. He was 91 years old when the World Cup began on 11 June in South Africa. Over three billion people worldwide watched this sporting event.
- The official match ball for the tournament in South Africa was called the Jabulani, which means 'to celebrate' in the local Zulu dialect. A new record was set for the number of goals scored in a World Cup with 145 goals scored in 64 matches.
- Famous pop star Shakira sang the 2010 World Cup song 'Waka Waka'. The music video of the song featured footage of Diego Maradona celebrating the famous Argentina win in the 1986 Mexico World Cup.
- Ireland requested FIFA to be allowed to participate in the 2010 World Cup as the 33rd team after they went out in the qualifying stage thanks to Thierry Henry's infamous handball that helped France qualify for the Cup. However, FIFA denied the Irish request.

Waka Waka (This Time for Africa) by Shakira

- One of the famous stars of the 2010 World Cup was the musical instrument known as the vuvuzela, played by the local spectators, which made a loud buzzing noise. The vuvuzela stole the show, but many players complained that they were distracted on the pitch by the loud noise.
- Hosts South Africa caused a massive upset when they beat France 2–1 in a group game. But South Africa drew with Mexico and lost to Uruguay to be placed third in the group. Sadly, the hosts missed going to the Round of 16 on goal difference.
- New Zealand were left cursing their luck as they had to exit the tournament despite not having lost a single match in the group stage. The Kiwis drew all their 3 group games and were third in the points table to eventually go out on goal difference. Their only consolation was that defending champions Italy finished last in the group.
- The South Africa World Cup had its share of upsets as Switzerland beat Spain in the group stages. Ghana reached the semi-finals after beating the United States while Germany humiliated Argentina 4–0 in another quarter-final.
- Uruguay reached the semi-finals after a long time. The national team jersey of Uruguay proudly displays four stars, each representing an achievement in the nation's football history. The first two stars symbolize their World Cup victories in 1930 and 1950 while the other two symbolize the Olympic gold medals won in the 1920s. Hopefully, they'll add a fifth star soon!

- The first time two brothers played against each other in a FIFA World Cup game was during the 2010 finals in South Africa. Jerome Boateng's Germany beat Kevin-Prince Boateng's Ghana 1–0.
- Over 7,50,000 litres of beer were sold within the stadiums during the tournament in South Africa. That's an astonishing 31,70,064 beers!
- The World Cup final saw two teams facing each other that had never won the World Cup before. The jinx in the finals haunted the Netherlands again as they lost to Spain 1–0 in extra time. Surprisingly, Spain won the World Cup scoring just 8 goals throughout the tournament.
- The World Cup final will remain infamous in history for the most yellow cards in a final. The Dutch players received 9 yellow cards, including a double to captain John Heitinga, resulting in a red card. The Spanish received 5 yellow cards. The previous record was 6 yellow cards in the 1986 World Cup final.
- In 2022, Sven-Göran Eriksson revealed that North Korea had approached him to influence the draw for the South Africa tournament and place them in an easy group. In 2010, Eriksson was a member of the FIFA Football Committee. When Eriksson refused, saying this was a criminal act, North Korean officials refused to believe him.

2014 World Cup Facts

- Brazil became the second nation to host the FIFA World Cup twice after Mexico. Brazil had hosted its first World Cup in 1950. The opening match between Brazil and Croatia had a record viewership of any opening match in World Cup history as over 42 million people tuned in to watch the game.
- The 2014 FIFA World Cup was the most-tweeted-about sporting event in history. Over 672 million tweets were sent during the one-month-long competition. Out of the twelve host Brazilian cities, eight are considered to be among the fifty most violent cities around the world.
- Although the sporting event had the most goals in World Cup history with 171 goals scored in 64 matches, it also had its share of upsets. Defending champions Spain were knocked out in the group stages, and footballing giants Italy and England went home early.
- Algeria became the first African nation to score 4 goals in a World Cup match. They achieved this feat against South Korea.
- Swiss striker Xherdan Shaqiri achieved a rare record of scoring the first-ever World Cup hat-trick entirely with the left foot. Shaqiri's goals helped Switzerland beat Honduras and progress to the Round of 16.
- For the first time in a World Cup, all the eight winners of the group stage progressed to the quarter-finals of the World Cup in Brazil. The tournament also saw 32

goals scored by substitutes, more than any previous World Cups.

- Colombian player James Rodríguez scored the most goals to win the Golden Boot with 6 goals, and German goalkeeper Manuel Neuer won the Golden Glove as the best goalkeeper of the tournament.
- Despite the splendid heroics of USA goalkeeper Tim Howard, who made as many as 16 saves in the match against Belgium in 2014, the USA lost the game 2–1 in extra time.
- Germany became the first European nation to win a World Cup in the Americas when they beat Argentina 1–0 in the final. This was Germany's fourth World Cup triumph but even more special as this was the first since they played after the reunification of West Germany and East Germany.
- After the Germans won the World Cup, Mesut Özil donated his entire €300,000 victory bonus to pay for the surgeries of twenty-three children in Brazil. Özil is definitely a footballer with a big heart!
- The 2014 World Cup was the most innovative till then as it saw the implementation of goal technology, the use of robots and drones for security and vanishing sprays by referees to mark free kicks.

2018 World Cup Facts

- Russia hosted the 2018 World Cup from 14 June to 15 July. Over 3.5 million fans crowded the stadiums, with an average attendance of over 47,000 per match.

- The FIFA World Cup is the most-watched sports event in the world. The global television audience in over 200 countries had a total viewership of 3.572 billion (that's 357.2 crore people). That means almost 50 per cent of the world's population watched the tournament. Wow!
- The maximum goals were scored in the Russia World Cup to date, with 169 goals scored in 64 matches. All teams scored at least 2 goals, which was a record. But it also featured early upsets as defending champions Germany crashed out in the group stages and Argentina exited in the Round of 16.
- England's Harry Kane was the top scorer of the tournament and received the Golden Boot while Luka Modrić of Croatia won the Golden Ball for the best player.
- The maximum number of penalties was awarded by referees in the 2018 World Cup as 29 spot kicks were taken throughout the tournament. Also, more goals were scored from set pieces than ever before. 9 winning goals were scored in the 90th minute or later.
- Egyptian goalkeeper Essam El-Hadary, nicknamed 'the High Dam', became the oldest player to appear at a World Cup aged 45 years and 161 days.
- The final saw France and Croatia lock horns in Moscow. In a match that saw the controversial use of VAR, France claimed their second World Cup title, beating Croatia 4–2. Croatia became the first team to lose in their maiden World Cup final appearance since the Netherlands in 1974.

France 4–2 Croatia | Extended Highlights | 2018 FIFA World Cup Final

- Apart from being prestigious, hosting the FIFA World Cup is a highly expensive affair for a country. The Russia World Cup cost a staggering US$14.2 billion. Before that, the 2014 World Cup in Brazil cost US$11.6 billion and Germany 2006 cost US$6 billion.

2022 World Cup Facts

- Qatar was the smallest nation to host the World Cup in 2022 from 20 November to 18 December. Qatar has a population of just 2.6 million with an area of only 4,416 square miles. An Asian country hosted the World Cup for the second time, and an Arab/Muslim country hosted the event for the first time.
- In another first, the World Cup was held in the winter in Qatar. Prior to this, the World Cup has always been hosted in the summer months. Qatar spent a mammoth $200 billion on infrastructure projects like stadiums, highways, and hotels.

- The 2022 Qatar World Cup sparked controversy due to allegations of corruption in the bidding process, concerns over human rights abuses involving migrant workers building the stadiums, and extreme heat conditions leading to the tournament being moved to winter for the first time in its history. These issues led to widespread criticism from fans, players, and human rights organizations globally.
- Only eight stadiums were used for the FIFA World Cup 2022 in Qatar. This was the lowest number of stadiums for the World Cup since the 1978 edition hosted by Argentina, who used only six stadiums. But in Qatar, less was more as all the stadiums were world-class.
- All eight venues in Qatar had air conditioning so that the players could play in good conditions and fans could experience a pleasurable viewing experience. The players would have liked that as they averaged a distance travelled of 9.65 km (5.9 miles) per game.
- A record of 172 goals was scored in this World Cup. Spain's 7–0 win over Costa Rica was their biggest victory in the World Cup. It was also Costa Rica's biggest-ever defeat in the World Cup.
- For the first time in the history of the World Cup, female referees officiated in men's matches in Qatar 2022. The three female referees selected for the prestigious job were Salima Mukansanga from Rwanda, Yoshimi Yamashita from Japan, and Stéphanie Frappart from France. A revolutionary move in sporting equality!
- When Portuguese superstar Cristiano Ronaldo scored against Ghana, he became the first player in the history

of the World Cup to score goals in five editions of the World Cup (2006, 2010, 2014, 2018, 2022).

- Canadian captain Alphonso Davies's goal against Croatia was Canada's first-ever goal at the World Cup. Davies celebrated in style as it was his 100th appearance for the Canadian national football team and he was the first Canadian player to achieve this feat.
- The host country has won 6 of the 22 World Cups so far. The only host nations that have failed to reach the second round are Qatar in 2022 and South Africa in 2010. But no host had ever lost the opening game of a World Cup till Qatar lost to Senegal.
- This was the first time in a World Cup that a UK national was not arrested throughout the tournament. Wonder if the Barmy Army were on their best behaviour in Qatar, or was it something else, like the lack of alcohol?
- The 2022 World Cup was England's best performance in any major tournament in terms of scoring goals. England scored 13 goals in Qatar, the highest tally in an edition of a major tournament like the World Cup and the Euro Cup.
- Spain's Gavi was the second youngest player to score at the World Cup when he found the net against Costa Rica. Gavi was aged 18 years and 110 days. Pelé is still the youngest, scoring against Sweden in the 1958 final aged 17 years and 249 days.
- Lionel Messi of Argentina became the first player to score in all the stages of the World Cup in a single edition. In Qatar, Messi scored goals in the group

stage, the Round of 16, quarter-final, semi-final and final. Messi also became the first footballer to win the Golden Ball at two World Cups.

- Asian giants Japan pulled off a shock win against fancied opponents Germany. But this is the first time Japan came from behind in the World Cup to win a match. When they had trailed before, they had lost 11 and drawn 2 of their matches.
- Mexico has qualified for the World Cup seventeen times, including Qatar, and this is more than any other country in the world. Sadly, Mexico has never won the World Cup despite hosting the event twice, in 1970 and 1986.
- For the first time in FIFA World Cup history, teams from all the continents in the world featured in the Round of 16 of the World Cup. That is indicative of just how competitive international football is today.
- Croatian goalkeeper Dominik Livaković became the third goalkeeper in World Cup history to make 3 saves in a World Cup penalty shoot-out. This was in the match against Japan. The first two goalkeepers to achieve this feat were Portugal's Ricardo in 2006 versus England and Croatia's Danijel Subašić versus Denmark in 2018.
- Lionel Messi became the player to be directly involved with the most goals in the World Cup since 1966. The 21 goals include 13 goals scored by Messi and 8 assists for Argentina. Messi also overtook Germany's Lothar Matthäus by making 26 appearances in World Cup matches, the most by any player.

- When Kylian Mbappé scored his 10th, 11th, and 12th goals at the Qatar World Cup, he became the fifteenth player to reach double figures in the World Cup in terms of goals scored. He was also the youngest to get there at 23 years and 363 days, beating German Gerd Müller's earlier record (24 years and 226 days).
- Kylian Mbappé also became the fifth footballer to score in two separate World Cup finals. The famous four who have done so earlier are Vavá (1958, 1962), Pelé (1958, 1970), Paul Breitner (1974, 1982), and Zinedine Zidane (1998, 2006). Mbappé has scored 4 goals in the finals of the World Cup, the most by any player.
- The final of the Qatar World Cup was the first in history that witnessed players from both teams score at least twice. Mbappé and Messi achieved this record

FIFA World Cup 2022 Logo

with the former scoring a hat-trick, the second man to do so in a final after Geoff Hurst of England in 1966.

- This was the last World Cup to feature a total of 32 participating teams. The 2026 edition of the World Cup is scheduled to have as many as 48 international teams competing for the ultimate footballing honour.
- The prize money for the champions of Qatar 2022 FIFA World Cup was a staggering $440 million, the most in any World Cup. No wonder that the highest ticket price in the World Cup was €48,802.
- The logo of the 2022 FIFA World Cup in Qatar was a unique ribbon that stood for both sand dunes, and infinity and harmony. The ribbon represented embellishments from ancient Arabic culture.
- England's 6–2 victory over Iran was their biggest-ever opening match win at a major footballing tournament like the World Cup and the Euro Cup. Manager Gareth Southgate notched up his 9th major tournament win with this match, the most by any English manager.
- When Enner Valencia scored the opening goal for Ecuador in the inaugural match in Qatar, it was the first time in the history of the World Cup that the opening goal was scored from the penalty spot.
- German player Youssoufa Moukoko became the youngest ever player to play for Germany in a World Cup game when he took the field in the match against Japan aged 18 years and three days.
- In their World Cup match against Spain, Costa Rica didn't have a single shot at goal. This is the second instance of a team failing to have a shot at goal in the World Cup after 1966. The first instance was Costa

Rica, again, against Brazil in 1990. That's a rare double!

- The most expensive player at the start of the World Cup was Frenchman Kylian Mbappé according to the online marketplace Transfermarkt. Mbappé's market worth was €160 million during the FIFA World Cup Qatar 2022. His performance was an indicator that his value would only increase.
- Wales's goalkeeper Wayne Hennessey became the third goalkeeper in World Cup history to receive marching orders after a red card in a match against Iran. The first was Italian keeper Gianluca Pagliuca against Norway in 1994 and the second was Itumeleng Khune for South Africa against Uruguay in 2010.
- Surprisingly, France was the first defending champion to win their opening game of a World Cup tournament after they beat Australia 4–1 since Brazil did it in 2006. None of the defending champions had won their opening game after 2006 till the latest World Cup.
- When Iranian Roozbeh Cheshmi scored a goal against Wales at 97 minutes and 56 seconds, it was the latest winning goal ever scored at the World Cup in regulation time since 1966 when the exact goal times are available to us.
- Enner Valencia of Ecuador became the fourth player in World Cups to score 6 consecutive goals in the tournament. The other three players to have done this are Eusébio for Portugal in 1966, Paolo Rossi for Italy in 1982, and Oleg Salenko for Russia in 1994.

- Although England has won the World Cup only once, it does have the rare record of the most goalless draws than any other nation. When England drew 0–0 with the USA, it was their 12th goalless draw at the World Cup. It was the USA's first-ever goalless draw in the World Cup.
- When Uruguay drew goalless with South Korea, statistics revealed that as many as eight different sides had goalless draws in their respective opening games of the 2022 World Cup. This is the highest number of goalless draws in the history of the World Cup.
- In the World Cup in Qatar, the prize for the noisiest fans was shared by Uruguay and South Korea. The Uruguayan and South Korean fans reached sound levels of a thunderous 131 decibels as they supported their respective teams.
- When they drew 1–1 with Spain, Germany created a unique record of not winning their first two group stage matches for the first time in their World Cup history. Germany was eliminated from the group stages at consecutive World Cups – 2018 and 2022.
- The 2022 World Cup saw 5 penalty shoot-outs, which was the highest in the history of the World Cup after penalty shoot-outs were introduced.
- Saudi Arabia created its own unique record at the 2022 World Cup when it received 14 yellow cards in the group stage itself. That's a maximum for any team during the group stages at any World Cup.
- When Japan beat Spain 2–1 in the group stage, they became only the third team in World Cup history to

be trailing at half-time and still winning 2 matches in a World Cup. The other two teams to achieve this are Brazil in 1938 and Germany in 1970.

- Spain dominated ball possession in the match against Japan. In fact, Japan only had 18 per cent ball possession, and this was the lowest for a team to win a World Cup match since 1966 as such precise data was only possible after that.
- Belgium were one of the favourites to lift the Cup and ranked No. 2 in the world after Brazil. They were placed with Croatia, Morocco, and Canada. But Belgium flattered to deceive as they failed to progress to the Round of 16 for the first time since 1998.
- Morocco became the first African nation to top their group since Nigeria did it first in 1998. But Morocco had 7 points, which is the most by any African team in the group stages. Morocco was also the first African country to reach the semi-finals of a World Cup.
- In another surprise, Cameroon created football history by becoming the first African team to beat Brazil at the World Cup. Before this match, African teams had lost all the 7 matches they had played against Brazil, conceding 20 goals. The times they are a changing.
- Lionel Messi made his 1,000th appearance for Argentina in the match against Australia. The occasion was special and demanded a goal. Messi did not disappoint, but this is the first time he scored in the knockout stages. His previous 8 goals in the competition were all in the group stage.
- When Olivier Giroud scored against Poland, it was his 52nd goal for France. He became the all-time top

scorer for France as he overtook the previous record holder, Thierry Henry, who had scored 51 goals.

- Brazil were 3–0 up against South Korea in just 29 minutes, and this is the fastest they have scored 3 goals in any World Cup match. This was also the second time in World Cup history that Brazil scored 4 goals in the first half, the first time being against Mexico in 1954.
- Brazil also used up all twenty-six members of their team with Weverton coming on as a substitute against Korea Republic. This is the first instance of any team using so many players in a World Cup match. Brazil certainly knows how to set the records.
- When Portugal defeated Switzerland 6–1, they created history as this was the victory with the largest margin in the knockout stages. Pepe became the oldest goal scorer in the knockout stages (39 years 289 days) and the second oldest goal scorer in all World Cup games after Roger Milla (42 years 39 days).

The Greatest Final Ever?! | Argentina v France | FIFA World Cup Qatar 2022 Highlights

- Argentina became the first team to win 5 penalty shoot-outs at the World Cup when they beat the Netherlands in the shoot-out after a high-voltage game. 15 yellow cards were flashed by the referee in the match where the Dutch equalized in the dying minutes.
- In 2022, England exited the World Cup at the quarter-final stage, and this was the seventh time they were eliminated in the quarter-finals of the World Cup, more than any other international side. England captain Harry Kane tied the record for most goals for England with Wayne Rooney with 53 career goals.
- When he scored against Croatia, Lionel Messi became the highest scorer for Argentina in World Cups with 11 goals. He was also the first Argentinian to score in 5 different matches in a single World Cup. Messi also became the only player in World Cup history to win the Golden Ball twice.
- Argentina won the World Cup for the third time after 1978 and 1986. The final was a thriller with Argentina and France tied at 3–3. The match went to penalties, where Argentina triumphed.

5

IMPORTANT INTERNATIONAL TOURNAMENTS AND LEAGUES

Conmebol Copa América Facts

- The Copa América was first played in 1916 and is the oldest international football tournament in the

The Copa América Trophy

world. Earlier, it was called the South American Championship as only South American teams took part. Recently, North American teams and Asian teams have also participated in the tournament.

- Argentina hosted the first edition of the Copa América in 1916 where, strangely, only four South American teams took part – Argentina, Brazil, Uruguay, and Chile. Ten countries have hosted the Copa so far, with Argentina hosting it the most – nine times.
- The Copa América was not held in 1918, 1924, 1928, 1932, and 1936 because of several pressing reasons such as war and organizational difficulties to host it.
- Argentina are the current defending champions of the Copa América, having lifted the Cup in 2021. The Copa has been held 47 times. Argentina and Uruguay have won 15 Copa América titles each, and Brazil has won Copa America 9 times.
- In 1942, Argentina registered the biggest victory in the history of Copa América when they hammered Ecuador 7–0.
- Despite playing in the Copa América since 1916, Chile had to wait for 10 long years before they registered their first match win in the Copa América. They had lost all their games before that.
- Chile also had to wait for as long as 2015 before they won their first Copa América title. Beginning in 1920, Chile has hosted the tournament 7 times and finally won when they hosted the Copa last in 2015. Claudio Bravo was the captain and Alexis Sánchez the star player of Chile.

- After almost a hundred years without the Copa América title, the Chileans made it 2 in two years when they triumphed again in 2016. The USA hosted this special edition of Copa América, which is the only one hosted out of South America known as the Copa América Centenario as it marked the 100th anniversary of the tournament.
- In 1983, Argentinian Jorge Burruchaga shared the Golden Boot award with Carlos Aguilera of Uruguay. Both the strikers scored just 3 goals each in the entire tournament. All 3 of Burruchaga's goals came in the group stages.
- In a noble gesture, guest nations from across the world have been invited to participate in the Copa América from 1993 onwards. Asian teams like Japan and Qatar have taken part in it. This move was to generate more interest in the Copa worldwide.
- The 2019 edition of Copa América was held in Brazil and featured teams from South America, as well as guest teams from Japan and Qatar.
- The guest nations in the Copa have also involved North American and Latin American teams. So far, none of the guests have won Copa América. Mexico became the closest to do so twice, finishing runners-up in 1993 and 2001.
- The worst team performance in the Copa América was by Ecuador in 1942. Not only did they lose all their matches in the group stage and finished at the bottom of their group table but scored only 4 goals while conceding 31 goals. This included a 12–0 drubbing at the hands of Argentina.

- Paraguay created Copa América history when they reached the finals of the tournament in 2011 without winning a single game. Paraguay drew all their 3 games in the group stage to progress as one of the best third-placed teams.
- Paraguay beat Brazil and Venezuela in penalty shoot-outs after goalless draws in the quarters and semis respectively to reach the finals. Their luck finally ran out in the final as Uruguay beat them 3–0 thanks to Luis Suárez.
- In the 1999 edition, Martín Palermo of Argentina created unique football history as he missed 3 penalties in a single match against Colombia in the group stage. That's a hat-trick of penalty misses and is a world record in all international matches to date.
- Amazingly, some of the legendary players from South America have not won the Copa América during their playing days. The list includes GOATs like Pelé and Diego Maradona.
- The Copa América had been elusive for Lionel Messi as well till he finally managed to win the tournament in 2021 with Argentina. But in the 2020 Copa América final against Chile, there was heartbreak for Messi as he missed a penalty in the shoot-out and Chile won the Cup.
- Messi was so distraught at losing the Copa América final and was criticized so much earlier by Argentinian fans for his failure to win a major tournament that he announced his retirement from the national team. Thankfully, he reversed his decision after a huge

campaign by Argentinian supporters. The rest is history!

- Many South American countries have hosted the Copa América ever since the tournament began. But it is Argentina that has hosted the maximum, with 9 editions, followed closely by Uruguay, who were the hosts on 8 occasions.
- The record for the largest victory in a Copa América game rests with Argentina. In 1942, they beat Ecuador 12–0.

UEFA Champions League Facts

The UEFA Champions League (also called the Champions League) is an annual club association football competition organized by the Union of European Football Associations.

- The Champions League trophy is nicknamed Ol' Big Ears because of its two large handles. The trophy is 73.5 cm in height and weighs 7.5 kg. That's almost the same weight as a big bowling ball.
- The Champions League trophy was designed by Jürg Stadelmann in 1967, and it took him as long as 340 hours to make. Stadelmann worked on a tight deadline as the trophy had to be completed on time and because he had to get married and leave for his honeymoon.
- The Champions League began in 1955, and since then, only 22 football clubs have managed to win it. Spanish club Real Madrid has won the Champions League the maximum number of times with 13 titles.

The Champions League Trophy

Real Madrid has also won the Champions League 5 times in a row.

- In comparison, English clubs have won the Champions League 14 times. The famous five English clubs include Liverpool with 6 titles, Manchester United with 3, Nottingham Forest and Chelsea with 2 titles each while Aston Villa has won once.
- However, it has to be considered that all English clubs were banned from playing in the Champions League for five years from 1986 to 1991 because of an unfortunate incident. It was a dark day in the Heysel Stadium with 39 people dead and 600 injured.
- A group of Liverpool fans attacked the Italian fans of Juventus by breaking down the barriers at the Heysel

Stadium that separated the fans of the two clubs. This triggered a wall collapse, causing the injuries and deaths. All the English clubs were banned as a result, and the rowdy fans were jailed.

- Dutchman Roy Makaay from German club Bayern Munich scored the fastest goal in Champions League history when he scored the first goal of the match against Spanish club Real Madrid in just 11 seconds. This record hasn't been broken in 12 years.
- The Champions League boasts of its own anthem that is, not surprisingly, titled 'Champions League'. The anthem was written by British composer Tony Britten and is played before each game in the Champions League to celebrate the gathering of so many national clubs for a sporting event.
- Tony Britten adapted German–British composer George Frideric Handel's 'Zadok the Priest' to create the Champions League anthem. The chorus of the song has the three official languages of the tournament integrated within it – English, German, and French.
- The 2019 UEFA Champions League final was a moment of great pride for English fans as two English clubs faced each other. It was the first time Tottenham Hotspurs reached the final, and they met Liverpool who were playing their 9th final. Liverpool lifted the trophy with a 2–0 victory.
- A club that lifts the Champions League trophy 5 times or wins 3 titles in a row is the recipient of the UEFA Badge of Honour. This badge is stitched on the player jerseys and displays an image of the trophy for which the clubs are competing to win.

- The number inside the trophy is also indicative of how many times the player's club has won the coveted trophy. So far, seven clubs have received the prestigious UEFA Badge of Honor – Barcelona, Real Madrid, Sevilla FC, AC Milan, Bayern Munich, Liverpool, and AFC Ajax.
- In 2012, Lionel Messi became the only player to score 5 goals in a single game for Barcelona against Bayer 04 Leverkusen. The record was tied by Brazilian Luiz Adriano in 2014 for Shakhtar Donetsk against BATE Borisov. In 2023, Norwegian Erling Haaland also equalled the record playing for Manchester City as he scored 5 goals against RB Leipzig.
- German football manager Thomas Tuchel is the first manager to reach the Champions League final in consecutive seasons with different clubs, leading both PSG and Chelsea there.
- When Thomas Tuchel was manager of Mainz, he went for dinner with Pep Guardiola thrice, who was then managing Barcelona. The two managers used the salt and pepper shakers and glasses to lay out their tactics on the dinner table before each other. That's a new one!
- Tuchel learned English when he was a professional football player in the early '90s when he was playing for a German team called Stuttgarter Kickers. His best friend in the team was South African–born striker Sean Dundee, who taught him the language. Dundee joined Liverpool in 1998 for £2m.
- Apart from English, Tuchel also speaks German, French and a little Italian and Latin. Pep Guardiola, on

the other hand, speaks five languages fluently: English, Spanish, Italian, German and Catalan. It helps to learn languages as a coach to broaden one's horizons and reach.

- Argentinian-born Alfredo Di Stéfano is considered the greatest Real Madrid player of all time. He won 5 European Cups and 8 La Ligas with Real Madrid. But the scenario could have been very different as Di Stéfano almost joined Barcelona before changing his mind.
- Lionel Messi of Barcelona is the fastest player to score 100 goals in the Champions League. He is also the all-time top scorer with 120 goals in 149 appearances.
- Scottish football club Dundee United has a 100 per cent win record against Spanish giants Barcelona. Dundee

Zlatan Ibrahimović

has played 4 professional matches against Barcelona and has won all 4. The Scots must be mighty proud to do something that the English haven't been able to achieve.

- Two legends of the game have never won the Champions League. The Brazilian Ronaldo is the first who played for four European clubs and failed. The maverick Zlatan Ibrahimović played for six teams that have won the Champions League, but he hasn't won it himself.
- Nottingham Forest is the only club in history that has been crowned European champions more times than they have been champions of their own country, England.
- Scotland is the only country that has had two teams from two cities in Dundee and Glasgow reach the semi-finals of the Champions League. Dundee did it in 1963 and Dundee United in 1984. Glasgow team Celtic reached the semis 4 times in 1967, 1970, 1972, and 1974 while Rangers did so once in 1960.
- Brazilian star Neymar da Silva Santos Júnior or Neymar Jr. formed a deadly attacking trio known as MSN during his Barcelona days with Lionel Messi and Luis Suárez. Neymar starred in Barcelona's 2014–15 Champions League triumph when they defeated Juventus 3–1 in the final with Neymar scoring a goal.
- Austrian manager Ernst Happel was the first coach who won the Champions League with two different clubs: Dutch club Feyenoord in 1969–70 and German club Hamburg in 1982–83.

- Arsenal player Theo Walcott has scored 15 goals in the Champions League, and this goal tally is more than European footballing heavyweights like Ronaldo Nazario, Zinedine Zidane, Miroslav Klose, David Villa, and Eden Hazard.
- The last time both European teams managed to reach the final of the Champions League without any foreign players in their starting XIs was the 1966–67 final between Celtic of Scotland and Inter Milan of Italy.
- Celestine Babayaro became the youngest player ever to appear in a Champions League game. In 1994, when he played for Anderlecht, he was only 16 years and 87 days old.
- In 2017, Roy Makaay of Bayern Munich scored the fastest goal in a Champions League game. He found the net in just 10.12 seconds against Real Madrid.
- Liverpool has won the Champions League title more times than any other English club, with 6 victories. Liverpool also had the largest margin of victory in a Champions League game when they defeated Beşiktaş 8–0 in 2007. Liverpool is the only team to win the Champions League without winning their domestic league that season in 2005.
- The highest-scoring Champions League final was in 2005 when Liverpool faced AC Milan. The game ended in a 3–3 draw after extra time. Liverpool eventually won on penalties.
- Portuguese star player Cristiano Ronaldo has won the Champions League as many as 5 times, with English club Manchester United and Spanish club Real Madrid.

- 2020 witnessed the highest-scoring match in the Champions League when German club Borussia Dortmund and Spanish club Sevilla faced each other. The match went in Dortmund's favour 5–4.
- 22 teams have played the Champions League final in the tournament's history. Out of these teams, only two teams have lost more finals than they have won. The first is Italian club Juventus and the second is Benfica from Portugal. Both have won 2 finals and lost 5.

UEFA European Championship/Euro Cup Facts

- The Euro Cup trophy is called the Henri Delaunay Trophy, having been named after the Frenchman who was one of the founding fathers of the tournament.

The Henri Delaunay Trophy, UEFA Euro Cup Trophy

In the Euro Cup, the top European countries battle it out for the title of champions of Europe.

- The highest-scoring game in the Euro Cup was played in 1960 and featured as many as 9 goals. Yugoslavia snatched a 5–4 victory over France in a thrilling match.
- In Euro 1968, hosts Italy faced the Soviet Union in Naples. Italy had had a horrific time in their last two meetings in international football against the Soviets, losing to them twice. This time, it was a goalless draw at the end of extra time.
- In 1968, the penalty shoot-out had still not been invented. After Italy and the Soviet Union's goalless draw, it was decided that a coin toss would decide the winner. It was a cruel way to decide the winner of a match.
- Italian captain Giacinto Facchetti and the captain of the Soviet Union, Albert Shesternyov, lined up for the toss. Facchetti called tails, which was the correct call. Italy went to the final and eventually won. This is the only match ever in the Euros to be decided by a coin toss.
- Euro 1968 hosts Italy were part of another controversy. In a first in the final of any Euro Cup, it was replayed after the final between Italy and Yugoslavia was tied 1–1 after extra time. The Italian team was stronger in the replay with the return of Gigi Riva and Sandro Mazzola and emerged as champions.
- In Euro 1976, Czechoslovakia had a dream journey to reach the final, where they beat West Germany 5–3 on penalties. This was the first victory by the Czechs

in a major tournament after they lost both the 1934 and 1962 World Cup finals.

- Even though Czechoslovakia had won Euro 1976, they had to qualify for Euro 1980 according to the rules then, instead of qualifying automatically. Czechoslovakia managed to qualify narrowly and were thus placed in the same group as West Germany. The Czechs had ten players from the victorious '76 side, while West Germany only had one.
- Czechoslovakia lost to West Germany in Euro 1980 as Karl-Heinz Rummenigge's goal won it for the West Germans. But the fact that the opening match of Euro 1980 was a rematch of the final of Euro 1976 is something that has never happened again in the Euros.
- The final of Euro 1996 was played between Germany and the Czech Republic, and the Euro 2000 final was played between Italy and France. Although these two finals were four years apart, they had a lot of similarities. For starters, both finals were decided by golden goals.
- In both the finals of Euro 1996 and Euro 2000, the winning teams came from behind to win the final. This was achieved in 1996 by Germany and in 2000 by France. In both the finals, the golden goals were scored by substitutes. Oliver Bierhoff scored the golden goal for Germany in 1996, and David Trezeguet did it for France in 2000.
- Euro 2004 also saw a similar incident to that of Euro 1980 with respect to the opening game. Both teams that played the opening game made it to the final as well in the same tournament. Surprisingly, Greece

defeated Portugal in both the matches. Greece won the opener 2–1 and the final 1–0.

- Germany has the best record in the European Championships as they have won 3 titles along with Spain. But where Germany are ahead is that they finished second in 3 tournaments as well. They have made the semi-finals 9 times in the Euros and are the only team to have participated at every tournament since 1972.
- England have a good qualifying record in the Euros but have never won the tournament. They failed to qualify in 1984 and went out in the group stages thrice in 1980, 1988 and 1992. Russia, Switzerland, and Sweden also have never won the Euros.
- Ruud Gullit was one of the most famous Dutch footballers. He captained the Netherlands team to victory at the UEFA Euro 1998. Along with Frank Rijkaard and Marco van Basten, he formed a lethal attacking trio. Gullit could play in all positions on the pitch and was nicknamed the 'Black Tulip' because of his famous braided hair.
- Only one player has played in 5 consecutive Euro Championships, and the honour belongs to Cristiano Ronaldo, who played in 2004, 2008, 2012, 2016, and 2020. Portugal won the Euro under his leadership in 2016 without winning a single game in the group stage and even though Ronaldo was injured in the final.
- Cristiano Ronaldo also holds the record for the most games played in the Euro with 21 appearances for Portugal. He is also the highest scorer in the Euro Cup

with 14 goals, beating Michel Platini's earlier record of 9 goals.

- No host nation has won the Euro in 37 years since France hosted it and won in 1984. In a funny fact, France were the hosts in 2016, but Portugal beat them in the final. In 2004, Portugal were the host nation but were beaten in the final by Greece.
- Spain became the only team to retain the trophy when they won the Euro in 2012, having won the earlier edition in 2008 as well. In comparison, Scotland and Northern Ireland have never progressed beyond the knockout stage.
- Didier Deschamps of France is the only man in the history of the Euro Cup to win the championship both as a player and a manager. It's a stupendous feat considering he's also managed to do the same in World Cups.
- Dmitri Kirichenko of Russia scored the fastest goal in the history of the Euro Cup. He found the back of the net just 67 seconds into the game against Greece in the 2004 edition of the tournament.
- The Euro Cup has witnessed some unbelievable upsets as complete underdogs have lifted the Cup. In 1992, Denmark won the tournament even though they didn't qualify for the tournament initially. Denmark qualified only after Yugoslavia was disqualified because of the country's break-up and ensuing warfare. Greece caused a major surprise by winning in 2004.

Bundesliga Flag

Bundesliga Facts

- Germany was a little late in forming their own professional football league compared to the English and Spanish, who've had their national top footballing divisions for more than a century. The late formation could also be attributed to Germany's political history. The first season of the Bundesliga began in August 1963.
- The Bundesliga was the league of West Germany as the East did not have a league of its own. After the unification of Germany, it became one league for one country. The first champions of the Bundesliga were Cologne.
- The first 7 seasons of the Bundesliga saw 7 champions – a different champion every year in Cologne, Werder Bremen, 1860 Munich, Eintracht Braunschweig, Nüremberg, Bayern Munich and Borussia Mönchengladbach (also called Gladbach). So, the Bundesliga was fiercely competitive in its early years.

- In the 1970–71 season, Gladbach became the first team to defend the Bundesliga title when they won the league for a second consecutive time. This was the era of a gripping contest between Gladbach and Bayern Munich. Between the 1968–69 and 1976–77 seasons, Gladbach claimed 5 titles and Bayern Munich 4.
- After this fierce rivalry with Gladbach, Bayern Munich emerged as the most powerful German club to date. They have won the Bundesliga a record 31 times and have never gone more than 3 seasons without winning the championship. Their career highlight has been from 2012–13 to the present.
- After Bayern Munich, it's a tie for second place with both Gladbach and Borussia Dortmund winning 5 titles each. Bremen have 4, Hamburg and VfB Stuttgart have 3 each, Cologne and Kaiserslautern have 2 each while 1860 Munich, Braunschweig, Nüremberg and Wolfsburg have 1 apiece.
- The individual with the most winners' medals in the Bundesliga is German goal-scoring machine Thomas Müller. He has a record 11 Bundesliga titles, since he started playing in the 2009–10 season. Robert Lewandowski is second with 10 titles won with Bayern and Dortmund.
- When it comes to coaches in the Bundesliga, Udo Lattek has the most Bundesliga titles to his name having won 8 managing both Bayern Munich and Gladbach in different stages of his career in the 1970s and '80s. Ottmar Hitzfeld is a close second with 7 titles won for Bayern Munich and Dortmund.

- The youngest coach/manager to win the title was 34-year-old Matthias Sammer when he led BVB to glory in 2001–02. On the other hand, 73-year-old Jupp Heynckes was the oldest manager in the Bundesliga when Bayern lifted the Cup in the 2017–18 season.
- Max Merkel became the first coach to win the Bundesliga twice. He won with 1860 Munich in 1965–66 and again with Nüremberg in 1967–68. Hennes Weisweiler was the first coach to win back-to-back titles with Gladbach in 1969–70 and 1970–71.
- Gerd Müller's haul of 365 goals from only 427 games in the Bundesliga is a record that will take some beating. He scored all his goals for Bayern Munich at a stunning rate of 1 goal every 105 minutes. Then, the striker, lovingly called 'Der Bomber', left for the USA aged 33 years.
- The second man on the list of top scorers in the Bundesliga is non-German. Polish striker Robert Lewandowski has scored a staggering 312 goals in 384 Bundesliga matches. That's 1 goal every 100 minutes. He is the top foreign goal-scorer after beating Peruvian Claudio Pizarro's record in March 2019. Sadly, he left Bayern in 2022.
- The city of Gelsenkirchen witnessed a strange situation when the stadium administration mistakenly scheduled a football and a handball match at the same time at the Parkstadion. Both the footballers and the handball players refused to budge, and so, both games happened on one field simultaneously. Four teams played with two balls.

Robert Lewandowski

- In Bundesliga history, there have been as many as thirty-two players with the last name Müller. None of them were related to each other though, and no prizes for guessing who the most famous Müller was.
- The record for the most goals scored by a player in one Bundesliga match belongs to Dieter Müller who scored 6 goals in Koln's 7–2 victory over Werder Bremen in 1997. Robert Lewandowski fell short by 1 goal when he came on as a substitute against Wolfsburg to score 5 goals in 9 minutes.

La Liga Facts

- The Spanish League or the Primera División, more famously known as La Liga, was founded in 1928. Nine different Spanish clubs have won La Liga ever since its inception, but Real Madrid has won the competition as many as 31 times.

- However, the first Spanish football league was the Campionat de Catalunya, or the Catalan football championship, established in 1901. After La Liga was created, the Catalan football championship co-existed with the new national league for a few years until it was ultimately cancelled in 1940.
- The first season of La Liga had one division known as the Primera División with ten clubs participating. In 1987, this number reached 20, and this is the usual number of teams. A deviation in the 1995–97 season saw 22 clubs taking part.
- Usually, 20 teams contest in La Liga and the three lowest-placed teams are relegated to the Segunda Division to be replaced by the top three teams in the Second Division. Of the founding teams in La Liga, only Real Madrid, Barcelona, and Athletic Bilbao have never been relegated.
- On 29 November 1899, Futbol Club Barcelona was founded by Joan Gamper. Since 1929, FC Barcelona has had 139 foreign players play for the team. Camp Nou, the Barcelona stadium, has the highest capacity in La Liga, with almost 1,00,000 seats.
- The football club of Barcelona derives its name from the capital city of Catalonia, which is an autonomous region located in northeastern Spain. The name originates from the Latin word 'Barcino', the name of an ancient Roman settlement that existed in the same region.

- Real Madrid was founded in 1902 and was originally named Madrid Football Club. In 1920, the word 'Real' was added, which means 'royal' in Spanish. This was after King Alfonso XIII granted the club permission to use the royal crown in its emblem.
- Real Madrid is one of the richest football clubs in the world, with a *Forbes* valuation of about $4.24 billion in 2021.
- Real Madrid's Santiago Bernabéu Stadium has a capacity of over 80,000 and is one of the most famous football stadiums in the world.
- Real Madrid has won the FIFA Club World Cup four times, which is the most wins by any club in the world.
- Real Madrid and Barcelona have dominated the La Liga since its inception. Both teams have won 60 of the total 89 trophies from the first La Liga season in 1929 till the present. They haven't finished in the top 2 positions in La Liga history on just 11 occasions.
- Luis Aragonés has served as the manager of 757 games in La Liga during his career as a manager. No other manager has managed to break the record.
- The youngest footballer ever to represent a La Liga team was Vicenç Martínez Alama. He was just 16 when he became Barcelona's youngest-ever footballer. On 19 October 1941, he played in the 'El Clásico' against Real Madrid, which Barcelona lost 4–3. Sadly, he retired at 28 in 1953 because of an injury.
- Real Madrid and Barcelona have a fierce rivalry in Spanish football. Matches between the two clubs are known as 'El Clásico'. The first El Clásico was played

in 1902 between the two teams, who have played each other over 240 times since then.

- The El Clásico between Real Madrid and Barcelona is considered by many as the biggest rivalry not only in La Liga but in the football world as well. It also has a deep cultural and historical significance in Spanish society with millions of spectators watching all over the world.
- Originally, the term 'El Clásico' was used for the Real Madrid versus Barcelona matches that took place only in La Liga. But today, it holds good for a match between the two teams even in the UEFA Champions League, the Copa del Rey or any other major tournament.
- Real Madrid is marginally ahead of Barcelona in recent head-to-head battles in the El Clásico by 90–87. But Barcelona is ahead in all-time matches with 106 wins to Real Madrid's 94. There were 58 draws between the two footballing giants.

Real Madrid versus Barcelona: El Clásico
Head-to-Head in All Major Competitions

Competition Name	Number of Matches	Real Madrid Wins	Barcelona Wins	Draws
La Liga	185	77	73	35
Copa del Rey	35	12	15	8
Supercopa de España	16	9	5	2

UEFA Champions League	8	3	2	3
Copa de La Liga	6	0	2	4
Copa de la Coronación	1	0	1	0
Exhibition matches	33	4	19	10
All	284	105	117	62

- The football rivalry between Barcelona and Real Madrid began as early as 1902, during one of their first meetings on a football field at a tournament held in honour of King Alfonso XIII.
- The hostility was fostered during the Franco era when

El Clásico Rivalry

Real Madrid was perceived as a symbol of Spanish nationalism, while FC Barcelona was the strongest expression of Catalan pride and identity. The El Clásico will be more than a football game for as long as the two regions don't see eye to eye.

- Confusion reigned when legendary Argentine footballer Alfredo Di Stéfano signed with both Real Madrid and Barcelona in the '50s thanks to a mistake by Di Stéfano's former club Millonarios Fútbol Club. Naturally, both the Spanish clubs wanted the legendary footballer in their team.
- The Spanish Federation mediated the transfer dispute of Alfredo Di Stéfano between Barcelona and Real Madrid. It ruled that the footballer would play four seasons in Spain, two for Real Madrid and two for FC Barcelona. This created a big scandal and a wave of protests by the fans of both teams.
- Owing to the fierce rivalry between the two teams in the El Clásico, it is rare for footballers to leave one club to join the other. However, in 1996, Luis Enrique moved to rivals FC Barcelona after playing five seasons for Real Madrid.
- In 2000, after spending five years at FC Barcelona, Portuguese star Luís Figo left the club to join Real Madrid. Another notorious transfer in El Clásico history is of star Brazilian striker Ronaldo. However, he joined Inter Milan first after spending the 1996–97 season at Barça for a then world record fee of $27 million.
- But Barcelona fans didn't like it one bit when Ronaldo Nazario joined Real Madrid in 2002 in the illustrious

company of Zinedine Zidane, Luís Figo, Roberto Carlos, Raúl, and David Beckham. This team was called the greatest football team of the century – the Galácticos.

- In total, only 33 football players switched sides from Real Madrid to Barcelona and vice versa in El Clásico's long history. Other prominent names include Gheorghe Hagi of Romania, Samuel Eto'o of Cameroon, and Argentinian footballer Javier Saviola.
- Barcelona suffered the heaviest defeat in El Clásico history in 1943 when Real Madrid thrashed them 11–1 at home. This was Real Madrid's record victory against their arch-rivals and took this rivalry to another level.
- The top goal scorer in the history of El Clásico is Lionel Messi for Barcelona with 21 goals in the contest over the years. Alfredo Di Stéfano is a close second with 18 goals while Cristiano Ronaldo has 16 goals. Messi is also the player with the most assists (13) and hat-tricks (2) in El Clásico.
- There have been a few rare occasions in El Clásico when fans have applauded a player from the opposing side. In the 1983 Copa de la Liga final at Santiago Bernabéu, Real Madrid fans paid tribute to Maradona's brilliance when he dribbled past the goalkeeper and waited for him to take his position again and defend his goal.
- In 2005, Ronaldinho received a standing ovation from Real Madrid fans for his splendid performance in a 3–0 win for Barcelona at the Bernabéu. On 21 November

2015, Andrés Iniesta of Barcelona received the same treatment.

- The El Clásico is such a big event in Spanish football that it has its own vocabulary. Real Madrid fans call themselves Merengues or Madridistas while the nicknames assigned to the players are Los Blancos and Galácticos. The Barcelona team is called Barça or Blaugrana and a fan is called Culé (backside) or Barcelonista.
- Canguelo is a term used by the Madrid sports press to describe Barcelona's fear of losing the league title to Real Madrid. Pegada is a word reflective of Real Madrid's traditional playing style. Villarato describes the situation where Madrid fans accuse Barcelona of winning thanks to favours from referees.
- Andoni Zubizarreta played in La Liga from 1981 to 1998 and holds the record for the most matches with teams like Barcelona, Athletic Bilbao, and Valencia Zubizarreta has an astonishing 622 appearances but strangely hasn't scored a single La Liga goal in any of these appearances.
- The least number of wins in an entire season in La Liga is two, and this record is shared by four clubs. In the 1997–98 season, Sporting Gijón created a record they won't be so proud of. They recorded the lowest points on the table in La Liga history with just 13 points.
- Cristiano Ronaldo has the highest number of goals in one season with 40 goals. Lionel Messi is the highest goal scorer in La Liga with 474 goals.

- The fastest hat-trick in La Liga took only 4 minutes and 43 seconds to score. Brazilian star Bebeto achieved the superlative feat playing for Deportivo La Coruña against Albacete in 1995.
- The record for the most goals scored in a game is jointly shared by Agustín Sauto Arana and László Kubala, who both scored 5 goals. Arana achieved the feat in 1931 when his team trounced Barcelona 12–1. 21 years later, Kubala replicated the effort as Barça thrashed Sporting Gijón 9–0.
- On 8 February 1931, Athletic Bilbao scored a famous 12–1 win over Barcelona, and this remains a record win in La Liga. The most goals in a single season were scored by Real Madrid. They scored 121 goals in the 2011–12 season.
- In the 1990–91 season, Atlético Madrid did not concede a goal in 13 consecutive games in La Liga, finishing second in the league that season. Atlético have won La Liga 11 times, and that includes a League

The Top 10 Most Thrilling El Clásico Matches (2000–2018)

and Cup double in 1996 as they won both the Copa del Rey and the Supercopa de España. They were also European Cup Winners' Cup champions in 1962.

- Lamine Yamal became the youngest-ever goal scorer in La Liga in 2023. He was just 16 years and 87 days old.

Serie A Facts

- In Italy, organized football began in 1898 as a regional competition under the supervision of Federazione Italiana Giuoco Calcio or the Italian Football Federation. In 1929, the Serie A was formed with 18 club teams across Italy taking part in the first season.
- Inter Milan, which was then known as Ambrosiana, won the first title, which is known as the Scudetto, meaning 'small shield' in Italian. During the 1980s and '90s, the Serie A was at its peak and Italian clubs were the most powerful in the world.
- During this golden era of Italian football, seven Italian clubs battled each other for top honours. They were Juventus, Milan, Inter, Roma, Lazio, Fiorentina, and Parma. Between 1983 and 2003, Serie A teams emerged as finalists in 13 European competitions and won 6 of them.
- Serie A has a tradition where a team that wins 10 Scudettos wears a star on their club's crest. That's why both Inter Milan and AC Milan have one star above their crests and Juventus has three stars.
- Under the able managerial skills of Antonio Conte and Massimiliano Allegri, Juventus have won 6 Scudettos

back to back, and their European record is most impressive with 2 Champions League final appearances in the last three years.

- But other than Juventus, the last Serie A teams to win the Champions League were AC Milan under Ancelotti and Inter Milan under José Mourinho. But both these Italian wins were almost a decade back.
- The record for the most goals scored by a player in Serie A is jointly held by Silvio Piola of Vercelli and Omar Sívori of Juventus. Both of them found the back of the net 6 times in a single game.
- The Serie A has produced more Ballon d'Or winners than any other football league in the world. This was before the merger with the FIFA World Player of the Year happened. Fourteen different Ballon d'Or winners have been produced by Italian clubs.
- Some of the players that won the Ballon d'Or for their exemplary performances at Serie A are Zinedine Zidane for Juventus, George Weah in his very first season at AC Milan, Marco van Basten (thrice) and Ruud Gullit (once) with AC Milan, and Ronaldo with Inter Milan.
- Sadly, Italian football and the Serie A were plagued by several corruption scandals from 2006 onwards. Clubs were accused of fixing matches and bribing referees to influence the outcome of a match. Juventus were stripped of their title and relegated to Serie B. Milan were penalized by 30 points as Lazio and Fiorentina were banned from European football.

EPL/ENGLISH FOOTBALL FACTS

Most Famous League

The English Premier League (EPL) is the most-watched football club league in the world in terms of viewership. It has over 4.7 billion viewers in over 200 countries.

Queen's Park in the FA Cup

The only Scottish club that has managed to reach an FA Cup final is Queen's Park based in Glasgow. They achieved this feat in consecutive years in 1884 and 1885 and sadly lost to Blackburn Rovers on both occasions. Two years later, the Scottish Football Association banned all Scottish teams from taking any further part in the FA Cup.

First Football League

The English Football League, which was formed officially in 1888, was the first-ever football league in the world.

First English Team Wins in Europe

The first English team to win a major European trophy was West Auckland Town FC when they won the Sir Thomas Lipton Trophy in Italy, defeating the Swiss, German and Italian club teams.

The English Champions of Copa del Rey

The only foreign club to win the Copa del Rey is English club Motherwell. In 1927, two foreign clubs were invited to participate in the tournament by the Spanish FA –

Motherwell and Swansea City. Motherwell emerged as champions by beating Real Madrid in the final.

The Special Trophy

A special version of the Copa del Rey trophy was donated by King Alfonso XIII of Spain to the members of the Motherwell team. Although Motherwell hasn't been able to replicate this kind of success ever, the trophy proudly decorates their trophy room today.

First Shirt Numbers

25 August 1928 was the first time shirt numbers were used in a game when Sheffield Wednesday defeated Arsenal 3–2. The numbers 1 to 11 were assigned to Sheffield Wednesday while Arsenal players wore the shirt numbers 12 to 22.

The First Black Player

Although Black players are an important part of leagues all around the world today, the first international Black footballer to make his debut in English football was Andrew Watson. He was born in British Guyana (now Guyana) and was the first non-white player to play the FA Cup.

Name Changes

English clubs Coventry City, Newcastle United, and Oldham Athletic originally had strange-sounding names till they were thankfully changed. The three clubs were known as Singers FC, Stanley AFC, and Pine Villa FC respectively.

Sunderland's Royal Luck

Sunderland is the only English club to have won a major domestic title in football under every sitting monarch in England since the invention of professional football. Strangely, they supported the Parliamentarians instead of the Royalists in the English Civil War.

Highest-Scoring Match

In 1936, the highest-scoring match in the history of English football happened when Arsenal beat Grimsby Town 9–1.

England's First Defeats on Home Soil

The Republic of Ireland became the first non-United Kingdom team to defeat England's football team on English soil when they won 2–0 on 21 September 1949 at Goodison Park. Hungary were the first foreign team to beat England when they won 6–3 at Wembley Stadium on 25 November 1953.

Scottish Glory

In the 1955–56 season, Hibernian of Scotland became the first British football club to reach a European Champions Cup semi-final.

The First Hundred Thousand Pounds Transfer

The first British footballer to be transferred for a hundred thousand pounds was Denis Law in June 1961 for a princely sum of £1,10,000 from Manchester City to Torino in Italy. A few weeks earlier, Jimmy Greaves was transferred from

AC Milan to Tottenham Hotspur for £99,999 and missed the mark by the narrowest margin possible.

Shilton's Lengthy Playing Career

An eight-year-old Gary Lineker went to watch the 1969 FA Cup final, where Leicester was playing Manchester City. The goalkeeper for Leicester was Peter Shilton. Lineker was Shilton's colleague for England for almost a decade. But he still retired from professional football three years before the great Peter Shilton.

Shilton for England

Peter Shilton's lengthy footballing career is illustrated by another interesting stat. Fifteen years existed between the end of Bobby Moore's international career and the beginning of Paul Gascoigne's. Peter Shilton played with both footballers for England.

West Brom Managers

The first names of West Bromwich Albion's managers from 1975 to 1988 were Johnny, Ronnie, John, Ron, Ronnie, Ron, Johnny, Nobby, Ron, and Ron. Whoever said, 'What's in a name?' should definitely do a rethink.

Football Company

In 1983, Tottenham Hotspur became the first football club in the world to become a public limited company.

No Yellow for Gary

English striker Gary Lineker made his English debut in 1984, scoring 48 goals in 80 appearances in an eight-year international career. Surprisingly, he never received a yellow card in his lengthy career.

The First Goal of the EPL

The first goal of the Premier League era was scored by Brian Deane, who was playing for Sheffield United as they managed a 2–1 victory over Manchester United in the inaugural match of the EPL on 15 August 1992.

Youngest Player–Manager

Jack Walker offered a 25-year-old Alan Shearer the player–manager job in Blackburn Rovers in a desperate attempt to keep him at the club when Shearer wanted to move. Shearer accepted the role, and the rest is EPL history. Alan Shearer has scored 260 goals – the most in EPL history.

Controversial Goal

In 1995, a study was conducted by the Engineering Department at Oxford University to conclude that Geoff Hurst's controversial winning goal for England in the 1966 World Cup final against West Germany did not cross the goal line fully. Too late to make amends!

Manager of the Month

Harry Redknapp is the only manager in the EPL to win the Premier League Manager of the Month Award for four different clubs: West Ham (November, 1998), Portsmouth (April and October, 2004), Southampton (March, 2005), and Tottenham Hotspur (August, 2009).

Bend It like Beckham

David Beckham scored a spectacular goal for Manchester United against Wimbledon from the halfway line, which is etched in the memory of football fans worldwide. But he actually scored the goal while wearing the boots of another footballer named Charlie Miller, who was a midfielder for Scotland and Glasgow Rangers.

The Predator Beckham

David Beckham was desperate to try out the new Predator boots from Adidas that had just been launched. Unfortunately, Adidas had only one pair of size eight available, which was Beckham's size. Those boots had been made for Charlie Miller and had 'Charlie' embroidered into the tongue of the boot.

Mourinho's Bright Future Quote

When coach Jose Mourinho told any of his players at the EPL that they had a bright future, it meant exactly the opposite. It simply meant that Mad Mourinho didn't want the player in his team. It's complicated.

Mourinho's Performance

Surprisingly, Mourinho didn't win a single Manager of the Month award in 2 of his 3 Premier League title-winning

José Mourinho

seasons. José Mourinho went an astonishing nine years without losing a home game.

Quickest EPL Goal

The record for the quickest EPL goal belongs to Ledley King, the former Tottenham Hotspur captain. King scored the goal just 10 seconds into the match against Bradford in the 2000–01 EPL season.

The GOLD EPL Trophy

In the history of the EPL, only one GOLD Premier League trophy has been awarded to a team. Arsenal were awarded this special trophy in the 2003–2004 season, where they did not lose a single match. That was the Arsenal dream team for sure.

The Three Young Turks

There are many players who have scored hat-tricks in the EPL. But only three players to score hat-tricks in a Premier League game were born after the English Premier League began in 1992. The three young Turks are Englishmen Raheem Sterling and Harry Kane, and Belgian player Romelu Lukaku.

Bale Does It All

Welshman Gareth Bale achieved the unique distinction of scoring a goal, assisting in a goal, scoring an own goal, and receiving a yellow card all in a single Premier League football game in 2013 when Tottenham played Liverpool.

Simon Says

Belgian goalkeeper Simon Mignolet played for Liverpool from 2013 to 2019. He had started as an outfield player in his younger days but switched to a goalkeeper when he was 15 years old. Mignolet speaks five languages and has a degree in politics. There's life after football for him.

Mata's Move

The competition between the top English Premiership Clubs is intense, and it is rare for players to move frequently from one top club to another in the EPL. Spaniard Juan Mata, for example, became the first player in EPL history to join Manchester United from Chelsea in 2014.

Using Their Heads

Two players in the EPL have scored a hat-trick by heading the ball into the net. Duncan Ferguson did it for Everton in a game against Bolton Wanderers in 1997, and Salomón Rondón achieved the same feat in 2016 for West Bromwich Albion against Swansea.

No Red for Lahm

Despite being a defender for Manchester United in the EPL, Philipp Lahm was extra careful in the box and has never received a red card in a game.

Youngest Player in the EPL

Harvey Elliot became the youngest footballer to play in the English Premiership League in 2019 when he made his debut for Wolverhampton Wanderers. Harvey had just celebrated his 16th birthday a month ago.

Man U Record

Manchester United is the most successful club in the history of English football. It has won a record 20 EPL titles, 12 FA Cups, and 3 European Cups.

The EPL Centurion

Ex-Manchester United player Ryan Giggs is the only footballer in the Premier League who has scored 100 goals in the competition without scoring a single hat-trick. Ryan Giggs has also been substituted 134 times. That's more than any other football player.

Gerrard Hates United

Liverpool and England midfielder Steven Gerrard has swapped his jersey with more than a hundred players during his career at the EPL. But he has never exchanged his jersey with a Manchester United player. That's one of the reasons Liverpool fans love him so much.

Chelsea's Unique Record

In a surprising fact, Chelsea have been relegated more times in the EPL than they have won the English Premier League. That's a great stat to know if you are not a Chelsea fan to poke fun at those that are.

Most Clean Sheets in the EPL

A clean sheet is when a goalkeeper doesn't concede a goal. Czech goalkeeper Petr Čech has kept the most Premier League clean sheets. He has kept 202 clean sheets in the EPL with 162 for Chelsea and 40 for Arsenal.

Least Goals Conceded

Chelsea holds the record for the fewest goals conceded in a single season. Chelsea conceded just 15 goals in the 2004–5 season. Petr Čech was guarding the goal for Chelsea.

Most Headed Goals

Peter Crouch holds the record for scoring the most headed goals in the history of the English Premier League. Crouch scored 53 goals using his head in his EPL career. Crouch played for 14 teams in a career that lasted for 19 years, scoring a total of 106 goals.

Best Playing Record

Manchester United player Ryan Giggs is the only Premier League player who has played in all the 21 seasons of his EPL career.

Fastest EPL Hat-Trick

The fastest hat-trick in the EPL was scored in just 176 seconds. Senegalese striker Sadio Mané achieved this remarkable feat on 16 May 2015 when Liverpool faced Aston Villa. Mané came off the bench in the 74th minute to score his hat-trick. He beat Robbie Fowler's record by 2 seconds.

Battle of Ys

In the FA Cup in 2021, when Yeovil Town faced Yate Town, it was the first-ever football match between two teams beginning with Y in English football.

Important International Football Leagues

6

THE GOATS

Pelé

- Pelé is considered the greatest footballer the world has ever produced. The Brazilian won 3 World Cups, 2 World Club Championships, and 9 Sao Paulo State Championships. He scored a mind-blowing total of 1,283 first-class goals, including 77 for Brazil.
- When he was 15 years old, Pelé was signed by famous Brazilian club Santos. He repaid their faith by scoring 4 goals on his league debut against FC Corinthians on 7 September 1956.
- Pelé was named after the American inventor Thomas Edison. His real name is Edson Arantes do Nascimento. Pelé's family gave him the nickname 'Dico'. The nickname Pelé came when he started going to school and when he used to mispronounce the name of the local Vasco da Gama goalkeeper Bilé. So, his classmate gave him the nickname Pelé, which stuck. Pelé has never liked his nickname, saying it sounds like 'baby talk'.

Pelé

- Pelé's first football team was formed with a group of friends from his poor Brazilian neighbourhood, and they called themselves 'the shoeless ones' because they didn't possess football boots. When he was young, Pelé used to play with a sock stuffed with paper as he could not afford to buy a football.
- Famous Brazilian forward Waldemar de Brito is credited with having discovered Pelé. He recognized Pelé's talent early on and was the one to take him to Santos. In a famous quote, de Brito had said of Pelé, 'He is going to be the greatest football player in the world.'
- Waldemar de Brito's words came true. A 17-year-old Pelé became the youngest winner of a World Cup. He

also scored 2 goals in the final against hosts Sweden to show that he had arrived.

- On 9 June 1957, Pelé scored his first hat-trick for Santos against Lavras. Pelé ran riot on 21 November 1964, scoring 8 goals in Santos's 11–0 win against Botafogo. Pelé scored 92 hat-tricks, 4 goals on 31 occasions, 5 on 6 occasions and scored 8 in the match mentioned above.
- In Brazil, Pelé is known as 'Pérola Negra', which means Black Pearl. The Brazilian government declared Pelé an official national treasure in 1961 so that he could never be transferred out of the country.
- 19 November 1969 was a historic day as Pelé scored his 1,000th career goal. Hundreds of fans ran onto the pitch to celebrate and mob the great footballer. It was over 30 minutes before the game could resume. Santos declared November 19 as 'Pelé Day' to celebrate the occasion.
- Pelé played his last football game on 1 October 1977 when Santos played New York Cosmos at the Giants Stadium. Pelé played the first half of the game for his American club and the second half for his first club Santos.
- In 1993, Pelé was inducted into the National Soccer Hall of Fame. Coca-Cola sponsors a Pelé museum on wheels in Brazil that travels throughout the country.
- Brazil appointed Pelé as minister of sport in 1995, and he served until 1998. In 1997, Pelé received an honorary British Knighthood. The International Olympic Committee (IOC) voted Pelé as Athlete of the Century in 1999.

- The best player in the world could not outdo his father in one department of the great game. Pelé's father once scored 5 headed goals in one game. Pelé was never able to replicate this feat as he only managed to score 4 headers in a single game.
- When Pelé played for the New York Cosmos, the club had to carry 25–30 jerseys of Pelé. That's because almost all of Pelé's opponents wanted Pelé's jersey as a souvenir after the game and wouldn't let them leave the stadium unless they were granted.
- Pelé holds the record for the most number of goals scored for the Brazilian team, and this record has stood for almost 40 years.
- In 2000, Pelé was named second in the BBC's 'Sportsman of the Century' award, only behind boxing legend Muhammad Ali. 'How do you spell Pelé?' the *Times of London* once declared. 'G-O-D'.
- Pelé has helped raise millions of pounds for charitable causes, including Great Ormond Street and Harlem Street Soccer. He is mentioned in the famous song 'Ghetto Superstar' by the rapper Pras.
- Pelé has also been a UNICEF goodwill ambassador and a United Nations ambassador after he retired from the game, working to protect the environment and fight corruption in Brazil.
- In 2000, FIFA decided to award a one-off Player of the Century award. It was decided that Pelé and Diego Maradona would share the award. Pelé famously said, 'If he thinks he's the best player of the century, that's his problem.'

Puskás

- Ferenc Puskás is the most famous footballer to play for Hungary and was one of the first stars. He played and coached the game on four continents. Puskás was born in 1927 in Józsefváros, Budapest, in a family of German descent. His father changed his name from Purczeld to Puskás after Ferenc was born.
- Puskás was a talented but temperamental player. In 1947, he was once banned for an entire year from playing in the national team by the Hungarian Football Federation because he beat up a Bulgarian footballer in Sofia.
- Puskás also refused to follow the instructions of the new coach of his club. Béla Guttmann left Budapest Honvéd as a result. Once, Puskás said harsh words to a linesman and was not allowed to play in the Hungarian Football League.
- Puskás shared a good rapport with the communist leadership of Hungary after World War II as football was a national passion. The national football team was privileged in the regime as they brought Western products back to Hungary and sold them. This was a profitable business behind the Iron Curtain.
- Puskás was so famous that he did not even need an appointment to meet the dreaded communist defence minister Mihály Farkas. So, he protected all his teammates and kept them out of trouble with the regime.
- Puskás scored 84 goals in 85 international appearances for Hungary and 4 international matches for Spain

and 514 goals in 529 league matches in Hungary and Spain. In 1952, he won the Olympic gold medal for Hungary and led them to the World Cup final in 1954.

- Many Hungarian fans accused Puskás and his teammates of throwing the match away to West Germany in exchange for Mercedes cars and money when Hungary lost the final. There were riots in Budapest for three days after this defeat and many are of the opinion that this led to the outbreak of the 1956 Hungarian revolution that ousted the communists from power.
- The Hungarian fans considered the coach Gusztáv Sebes and the captain Ferenc Puskás as the main culprits for the World Cup final debacle. When the 1956 revolution was crushed by Soviet tanks, the Hungarian football team was in Spain. The communist leadership ordered them to return to Hungary, but Puskás and his team refused.
- The Hungarian team began a European tour, playing football matches for money, and also travelled to Brazil. The Magical Magyars were received everywhere as superstars, and most did not return to Hungary, including Puskás. Hence, the communist government branded Puskás as a traitor.
- Puskás decided to smuggle his wife and four-year-old daughter out of Hungary before the Communist leadership used them to blackmail him to return to Hungary. After several efforts to cross the Austrian border on foot resulted in failure, human smugglers were hired to reunite them with Puskás in Vienna in December 1957.

- Puskás moved to Spain in 1958, two years after the Hungarian Revolution, and joined Real Madrid to become one of their most successful players. He scored 7 goals in two European Champions Cup finals and was part of the winning team in three European Cups. He also won 10 national titles including 5 Hungarian and five Spain Primera División titles.
- Puskás is the fourth-best striker of all time in terms of goals scored. He scored 806 goals in 793 official games. Any list of legendary footballers is incomplete without Ferenc Puskás.

Maradona

- On 30 October 1960, Diego Armando Maradona was born on the outskirts of Buenos Aires, Argentina. In 91 appearances for Argentina, Maradona scored 34 goals. Maradona played in four World Cups and guided Argentina to a famous victory in Mexico '86.
- As a 15-year-old, Maradona made his professional footballing debut for Argentinos Juniors on 20 October 1976. Years later, Argentinos Juniors named their stadium after Maradona, calling it Estadio Diego Armando Maradona in an ultimate honour.
- Maradona made his international debut against Hungary at age 16 on 27 February 1977 at La Bombonera, a stadium in Buenos Aires. He was also part of the Argentina youth squad that won the 1979 Youth World Cup in Japan.
- In 1978, ex-England defender Phil Neal praised an 18-year-old Maradona, saying, 'The kid is just unbelievable – he is the best I have ever seen.'

Diego Maradona

- Maradona later moved to Argentinian club Boca Juniors and helped them win the league championship in 1982 before his big move to Spanish giants Barcelona. But his stay at Barcelona wasn't pleasant, and Maradona moved to Serie A club Napoli in 1984.
- Maradona transformed an ordinary club like Napoli into a footballing force, helping them win their only two Serie A titles to date in 1987 and 1990. Napoli also won the UEFA Cup in 1989. No wonder Maradona is revered in the city of Napoli!
- Maradona had a great partnership with Italian Bruno Giordano and Brazilian Careca, which was responsible for Napoli's second Serie A win in 1989–90. The trio was called the 'Ma-Gi-Ca' (Magic) front line.

- Once, while playing Real Madrid, Maradona dribbled past goalkeeper Agustín and defender Juan José before putting the ball in the net. He was applauded by the Real Madrid fans for the goal – one of the few players to have received such an ovation.
- Maradona holds the record for being fouled the most in a World Cup – 53 times during the 1986 Mexico World Cup. He also holds the record for being fouled the most in a single World Cup game. In 1982, Italy fouled him 23 times.
- Maradona has made 21 World Cup appearances for Argentina and has captained Argentina on 16 occasions in the World Cup. He holds the record for most World Cup appearances as a captain of any country.
- Maradona led Argentina to World Cup glory in 1986, beating West Germany 3–2 in the final. He also won the Golden Ball for being the tournament's best player.
- Maradona idolized Che Guevara and Fidel Castro. He was also good friends with Cuban leader Castro. As a mark of respect, Maradona had a tattoo of Che Guevara on his arm and a picture of Fidel Castro tattooed on his left leg.
- Maradona scored with his hand against England in the 1986 World Cup quarter-final. He termed it as 'the goal scored a little bit by the hand of God, a little by the head of Maradona'. His second goal saw him dribble past English defenders to beat Peter Shilton. FIFA called this the Goal of the Century.
- Referring to the dispute with England about the Falkland Islands, Maradona said after beating

England, 'It was as if we had beaten a country, more than just a football team.' Former England manager Sir Bobby Robson famously said, 'With Maradona, Arsenal could have won the World Cup.'

- Maradona married Claudia Villafañe on 7 November 1989 in Buenos Aires, but his marriage fell apart as the pair divorced in 2004.
- When Argentina manager Carlos Bilardo was asked once to name his starting XI in 1990, he famously said, 'Maradona and ten others.' Sadly, 'Maradona and ten others' lost the final 1–0 to the German eleven in the final of the 1990 World Cup.
- Maradona's downslide began because of his drug addiction. He had to leave Napoli in 1991 after failing a drug test for cocaine. In the 1994 World Cup in the USA, Maradona played only 2 games, scoring a goal against Greece. But he was sent home in disgrace after failing a doping test.
- In 1998, fans started a 'Church of Maradona' in Buenos Aires. The year is marked by Maradona's birthday every year. 30 October 2020 was 60 D.D. (despues de Diego or 'After Diego').
- In 2000, Maradona published his autobiography *Yo Soy El Diego*, meaning 'I Am The Diego'. He donated the proceeds of the Cuban royalties of his book to the Cuban people as a gesture of love.
- Maradona began hosting a talk show on Argentinian television in 2005. Despite their intense rivalry and occasional war of words, Pelé was Maradona's main guest on the very first episode of the show.

- In December 2007, Maradona presented a signed shirt with a message of support to the Iranian people. The shirt is proudly displayed in the museum of the Iranian Ministry of Foreign Affairs.
- Serbian filmmaker Emir Kusturica was a big Maradona fan. He made a documentary about Maradona, which premiered at the Cannes Film Festival in 2008.
- In October 2008, Maradona was appointed as the manager of Argentina's national team. His managerial debut for Argentina was on 19 November 2008 when Argentina beat Scotland 1–0 at Hampden Park.
- But Maradona was criticized heavily as Argentina suffered their worst-ever defeat with him as manager. Bolivia thrashed Argentina 6–1 in a World Cup qualifying game. But Argentina still managed to qualify for the World Cup, and Maradona verbally abused his detractors. FIFA banned him for two months for the outburst.
- In a war of words, Pelé said during Maradona's stint as Argentina's manager, 'But it isn't Maradona's fault. It is the fault of whoever put him in charge.' Maradona shot back saying, 'Pelé should go back to the museum. And stay there.'
- As a tribute to Maradona, the authorities at the Azteca Stadium built a statue of him scoring the 'Goal of the Century' and placed it at the entrance to the stadium.
- Once, the Argentine Football Association put in a request to FIFA to retire the No. 10 shirt in honour of Diego Maradona. The request was denied by FIFA. No one is bigger than the game after all!

- In 2009, Italian officials revealed that Maradona owed them €37 million (£32.2m). More than half the sum was interest on the original debt. It is not known what Maradona said to the Italian officials, but we would have loved to hear it.
- Maradona averaged 0.526 goals per game in domestic club competitions. Strangely, he is only the fifth-highest goal scorer for Argentina, behind Lionel Messi, Gabriel Batistuta, Sergio Agüero, and Hernán Crespo.
- Maradona is the only player in the history of football to have broken the record transfer fee twice. He and Messi are the only players to have won the Golden Ball at both the FIFA U-20 World Cup and the FIFA World Cup.
- Maradona visited Ali Bin Nasser, the Tunisian referee, on 17 August 2015 and paid him tribute by presenting a signed Argentine jersey. Nasser was the referee in Argentina's '86 quarter-final against England when Maradona scored the infamous 'Hand of God' goal and the famous 'Goal of the Century'.

Diego Maradona's Top 5 Goals | FIFA World Cup

- Diego Maradona breathed his last after a massive heart attack on 25 November 2020 – the anniversary of both footballer George Best and Maradona's good friend Fidel Castro.

Beckenbauer

- German Franz Anton Beckenbauer is a living football legend who was nicknamed der Kaiser because of his elegant play, midfield dominance and leadership skills on the pitch. Once, in 1968, during a friendly match in Austria, Beckenbauer posed for a portrait next to a sculpture of former Austrian emperor Franz Joseph I. After that, fans and the media nicknamed him 'der Kaiser'. The nickname was also on account of his first name 'Franz'.

Franz Beckenbauer

- Beckenbauer helped Germany win almost all major international trophies, both as a player and a manager. Later, he served as an able administrator and enjoys iconic status in Germany as well as other parts of the footballing world.
- Beckenbauer fell in love with football at an early age and joined SC Munich in 1954 when he was only nine years old. His father did not like this affinity for football, but young Franz was unstoppable just like he was on the field. In 1959, the 14-year-old Beckenbauer joined German giants Bayern Munich.
- Controversy erupted over a pregnant girlfriend in 1963, and an 18-year-old Franz Beckenbauer was banned from the West German National Youth Team. Coach Dettmar Cramer acted as a mediator, and Beckenbauer found his way back into the side.
- Beckenbauer scored 4 goals in the 1966 World Cup and was a versatile player. He could play in many positions, like central defence, defensive midfield or centre midfield. But he was his best at playing the sweeper role and revolutionized this position.
- Franz Beckenbauer is credited with the creation of the position of the modern sweeper or 'libero' in football. This was a modern approach to defending, and the libero spot remains one of his most memorable legacies to the beautiful game.
- Apart from his victories as German captain and manager in international tournaments, Beckenbauer took his club Bayern Munich to new heights, too. Under his captaincy, Bayern won three league titles

back to back from 1972 onwards. They also enjoyed three straight European Cup wins at the same time.

- In his 584 appearances for Bayern Munich, Beckenbauer scored 75 goals. In 1977, Beckenbauer parted ways with Bayern Munich to join the New York Cosmos in the United States Soccer League. He was a teammate of Pelé in this club, which was impossible to beat with these two legends in the team.
- Pelé had been Beckenbauer's hero since the 1970 World Cup. So, it was a great honour to play alongside him. They together helped the New York Cosmos win the North American Soccer League thrice.
- Beckenbauer was inducted into the US National Soccer Hall of Fame. He represented New York Cosmos for four seasons before deciding to head back to Germany. He joined Hamburger SV and played two seasons at this German club before announcing his retirement. Hamburger SV won the league in his last season.
- Strangely, Beckenbauer played 38 games in two seasons for Hamburger SV but didn't score a single goal. In comparison, he represented West Germany 103 times and scored 14 goals.
- In 1993, he was appointed the interim manager of Bayern Munich, and Beckenbauer took to the new role like a fish to water, guiding his former club to the league title that season. Three years later, Bayern appointed him as a temporary manager again, and this time, he led them to a UEFA Cup victory.
- Franz Beckenbauer's resume as a manager is impressive to the core with five Bundesliga titles, three European Cups, a World Cup, and a European Championship.

Very few have made the transition from a great player to a great manager, and the name of Franz Beckenbauer tops that special list.

- Franz Beckenbauer was also a top-level football administrator who was president of Bayern Munich for 15 years. He spearheaded Germany's 2006 World Cup bid as vice president of the German Football Association. When the World Cup was underway, Beckenbauer watched 46 of the 64 matches live thanks to a sponsored helicopter at his disposal.
- The progressive Franz Beckenbauer is pretty active on social media. On Instagram, he can be found with the username @franzbeckenbauer, with 17.7K followers. His X (formerly Twitter) account name is 'Franz Beckenbauer', with 1.1 million followers. His 'Franz Beckenbauer' Facebook profile has 380k followers. Not bad for an old-timer, eh?

Platini

- French footballer Michel Platini was one of football's all-time greats. Born to Italian-born parents, Platini signed his first professional footballing contract with Nancy just after the 1976 Montreal Olympics. He led Nancy to victory in the 1978 French Cup against Nice by scoring the only goal of the match.
- Leading French club PSG expressed an interest in Platini after his contract with Nancy ended. But Platini chose to join AS Saint-Étienne on a three-year contract.
- Platini has played 72 games for France, including 49 as captain of the French team, between 1976 and 1987

and has scored 41 goals. This goal-scoring record was broken by Thierry Henry and recently by Olivier Giroud.

- Platini won the prestigious Ballon d'Or thrice in a row in 1983, 1984, and 1985. He was made a Chevalier of the Légion d'honneur in 1985 and an Officier in 1998 to honour his efforts for the game.
- Platini is a member of both the English and Italian Football Halls of Fame. He was a key member of the French team that won the 1984 European Championship, where Platini was the top scorer and also received the Best Player award.
- Platini retired from professional football in 1987 and became the coach of the national team for four years in 1988. Under Platini, the French team had a 19-match unbeaten streak. Platini was voted Manager of the Year by the World Soccer Awards.
- France was among the favourites to win the 1992 World Cup with Platini as coach and talented young players like Eric Cantona, Laurent Blanc, and Didier Deschamps. But to everyone's surprise, they went home after the group stage. This prompted Platini to resign as the coach.
- Platini co-chaired the organizing committee for the 1998 FIFA World Cup, which France won for the first time. He quickly rose through the ranks of the FIFA football administration, becoming chairman of the FIFA Technical and Development Committee and vice president of the French Football Federation in 2006.
- Platini was president of UEFA, the global governing body of European football, from 2007 to 2015. But

he was barred from football for eight years over corruption charges. Platini managed to reduce the sentence to four years and returned to football in 2019.

Cruyff

- Hendrik Johannes Cruijff or Johan Cruyff was a legendary Dutch footballer who became a footballer as a tribute to his father. Cruyff was only 13 years old when his father passed away. Most boys would have given up on their footballing dream, but his shock made Cruyff even more determined.
- Cruyff was helped in his quest to become the greatest Dutch footballer of all time thanks to the efforts of his mother, who supported the family financially, working

Johan Cruyff

as a cleaner. Cruyff's stepfather also inspired him to chase his dream.

- In his early teens, Cruyff was also a talented baseball player. He was not only part of Ajax's youth football academy but also a part of their baseball section, displaying great talent as a catcher and pitcher. But he had to quit baseball for football when he was 15.
- Cruyff was a man who always had his way no matter the circumstances. Even his move to Spain was rather controversial. Ajax wanted to sell him to Real Madrid, but Cruyff wanted to join Barcelona. He relished the challenge of playing at Barcelona because Madrid was a more superior club then.
- Cruyff ultimately had his way and joined Barcelona when they were plagued by mediocrity. Thanks largely to Cruyff, Barca scaled new heights, and that's why the Dutch footballer is revered in Spain as much as he is in Holland. He was Barcelona's greatest player till a man named Lionel Messi arrived there much later.
- The 'Cruyff turn' was the Dutchman's signature move when he turned defenders inside out by either dropping his shoulder or twitching his bum. But the name was a reference also to his strange turns at training when he would suddenly disappear to be found smoking in the dressing room or doing John Cleese walk impersonations.
- For a footballer, Cruyff was a heavy smoker. But strangely, this never affected the genius's performance. In the 1970s, Cruyff was petrified by the prospect of smoking being banned in public places. But he was a

relieved man when this prophecy finally came true as he had given up smoking by then.

- During his stint at Barcelona, Cruyff and his family were once held hostage at gunpoint by a group of kidnappers in 1977. They tied up his wife in front of his children at Cruyff's residence. Luckily, Cruyff managed to escape and was guarded by authorities after that.
- Because of the unfortunate incident of the hostage situation in Barcelona, Cruyff did not participate in the 1978 FIFA World Cup as he feared for his family's safety and did not want to leave them alone. The Netherlands finished runners-up in Cruyff's absence.
- Dutch fans firmly believe that they would have won the elusive World Cup had their greatest footballer been present. To date, the Netherlands have never managed to win the World Cup.
- After his retirement from the game, Cruyff became the manager of Barcelona in 1987. Cruyff had named his cat General Franco, and with the move as Barça manager, had to change the cat's name. He changed it to Alfredo di Stéfano, the Real Madrid legend!
- Cruyff guided Barcelona to their first European Cup victory in 1992 as they beat Sampdoria in the final at Wembley. To celebrate the occasion, Cruyff took his teammates to the notorious Blind Beggar Pub in Whitechapel, which was a strange choice of venue.
- The Blind Beggar Pub was made infamous in the '60s when Jack 'The Biscuit' McVitie was murdered here by fellow gangster Ronnie Kray. Barcelona's celebrations here threatened to turn ugly when Ronald Koeman

split dreaded gangster 'Mad' Frankie Fraser's pint. But Cruyff cooled things down by buying Fraser another pint and some crisps.

- Johan Cruyff was also famous for his funny quotes that many Dutch people used in their daily lives. These are known as Cruyffisms, and the most quoted one was, 'De bol is rond,' meaning, 'The ball is round.' Others include, 'Every advantage has its disadvantage,' and 'Without the ball, you can't win.'
- Johan Cruyff's son, Jordi Cruyff, was not a legendary footballer like his father but was still good enough to represent Holland, Barcelona, and Manchester United at various stages of his career. But controversy followed Cruyff even when he named his son.
- Cruyff was advised by the registrar to change his son's name because the patron saint of Catalonia is named Jordi. But once Cruyff had made up his mind, no one could change it. So, despite all opposition, Cruyff named his son Jordi. He had his way like he always did in life.

Eusébio

- Born and raised in the African country of Mozambique, the legendary footballer Eusébio da Silva Ferreira joined Portuguese club Benfica in 1961. Soon, he became a part of the Portuguese football team to be one of the legendary champions of the game. He was named the 'Black Pearl' and the 'Black Panther'.
- In an astonishing record, Eusébio was the top scorer for the Portuguese League every year from 1964 to

1973. Thanks to his efforts, Benfica won 10 league championships and 5 Cup victories. Eusébio is one of the footballing legends never to have won a World Cup.

- Before joining Benfica, Eusébio played for Sporting Clube de Lourenço Marques for two seasons. He was spotted by a scout who was a former Juventus goalkeeper. The scout recommended Eusébio highly, but Eusébio's family refused Juventus's offer.
- Eusébio was an exceptional footballer who was both skilful and fast when he was 18 years old. He was ambidextrous; playing skilfully with both legs and could cover 100 m in less than 11 seconds. Former Brazil player José Carlos Bauer introduced him to Benfica when talks with Brazilian club São Paulo didn't materialize because of money.
- Even though Benfica were eager to hire Eusébio, the going was tough as they had to first convince Eusébio's mother. This was managed after Eusébio's salary was paid to his mom. After Eusébio arrived in Lisbon, he was in hiding for twelve days because Benfica wanted to protect this rare talent.
- Eusébio began his career with his local club, Sporting Clube de Lourenço Marques, in Mozambique, which was affiliated with Sporting Lisbon, and they were displeased with him joining Benfica. After being flown to Portugal, Eusébio was given the codename Ruth Malosso and hidden away lest he be kidnapped by Sporting.
- Eusébio's debut for Benfica was on 23 May 1961, against Atlético Clube de Portugal in a friendly match.

By his second season, Eusébio had become a star, scoring 12 goals in 17 matches, taking Benfica to the third position on the league table.

- Eusébio scored 727 goals in 715 games for Benfica, which is an impressive record. Thanks to him, Benfica also won 5–3 against the powerful Real Madrid, with Eusébio scoring a brace.
- Eusébio played 64 matches for Portugal and scored 41 goals. This was a national goal-scoring record for a long time till Pauleta beat the record. But the highlight of his international career was definitely the 1966 World Cup, where Portugal was in the Group of Death with Bulgaria, Hungary, and Brazil.
- Thanks to Eusébio's heroics and Pelé's injury, Portugal beat Brazil, as well as all the other teams in their group. In the match against North Korea, who had beaten Italy earlier, Eusébio came to the rescue by scoring 4 goals when his team trailed by 3 goals to register a famous win.
- Portugal faced England in the semi-finals of the 1966 World Cup, and English defensive midfielder Nobby Stiles marked Eusébio effectively and prevented him from reaching England's goal. Eusébio still managed to score a goal through a penalty, but England won 2–1.
- Although Portugal beat the Soviet Union and earned third place in the 1966 World Cup, there was no denying that Eusébio was by far the best player of the tournament. He was also the first great African footballer.

- In the final seconds of normal time in the match against Manchester United in the European Cup Final at Wembley, Eusébio had a great chance to win the game for Benfica. But his effort was foiled by a great save from United keeper Alex Stepney. The great Eusébio applauded the goalkeeper and shook his hand.
- After spending most of his career with Benfica, Eusébio played for smaller Portuguese teams like Beira-Mar and União de Tomar. Then he moved to North America, where he played for three other teams called Boston Minutemen, Toronto Metros-Croatia, and Las Vegas Quicksilvers. But he was forced to retire in 1979 because of injuries.
- Post-retirement, Eusébio went into coaching and joined the technical committee of the Portuguese national football team. Eusébio died because of heart failure on 5 January 2014, and the entire footballing world went into mourning as he was loved and respected all over the world.
- The Portuguese government declared three days of national mourning after Eusébio's death. Several football stars like Cristiano Ronaldo, José Mourinho and FIFA president Sepp Blatter paid their respects to Eusébio's tomb, which is now in the National Pantheon in Lisbon. Three days later, Eusébio's statue was transformed into a memorial at the Perca Centenarium. A year later, the avenue of the Estádio da Luz was renamed after Eusébio da Silva Ferreira.
- Benfica players paid their last respects to the footballing legend who was responsible for the club's phenomenal success in the unique way that only footballers can.

They put Eusébio's name on the backs of their jerseys when they played.

Zico

- Brazilian Arthur Antunes Coimbra was a legendary footballer, famously known as Zico. He was born on 3 March 1953 in the neighbourhood of Quintino Bocaiuva in Rio de Janeiro, Brazil. Zico often bunked school to play football on the streets as people gathered to watch him play.
- 'Zico' is an abbreviation of his childhood nickname. Arthur Antunes Coimbra was called Arthurzico by his family. This name was shortened to Zico later and stuck. His other nickname, O Galinho – the Rooster – was given by Brazilian radio commentator Waldir

Zico

Amaral, inspired by the quiff hairstyle young Zico sported.

- Zico's first team was a local futsal team named Juventude, which was run by his elder brother and his friends. He also played for a club named River Futebol Clube on Sundays, where he shot into prominence when he was 14 years old.
- A 14-year-old Zico scored 9 goals in a match, and people realized his talent. At the urging of a radio reporter called Celso Garcia, Zico's father took him for a trial to the top Brazilian club, Flamengo. It was 1967.
- The Flamengo Youth Academy almost refused to accept Zico because they felt he was too thin and physically weak to play football. They put him on a nutrition and gym exercise regimen, and this was a smart move. Zico did wonders for Flamengo later.
- As a member of the senior Flamengo team, Zico helped them win 3 of their 6 Brazilian League titles and 1 FIFA Club World Cup.
- Zico was the third professional player in his family of Portuguese origin. His elder brother, Edu, was a talented midfielder who was unlucky not to be picked in the great Brazilian side of the late 1960s and early '70s. Edu managed the Brazilian team for 3 games in 1984.
- Zico was literally worshipped by Flamengo fans. But he never liked the strange practice by groups of supporters who jokingly wished each other 'Happy Christmas' to celebrate Zico's birthday on 3rd March.

- Zico has scored more goals at the legendary Maracanã Stadium than any other footballer. He has a staggering 333 goals in 435 games at the stadium in Rio. Even though Zico was a midfielder, he was a prolific goal scorer.
- Zico played for the Italian club Udinese Calcio from 1983 to '85, turning down offers from bigger clubs like Turin, AC Milan, and Roma. Udinese Calcio has a supporters' group named after Zico who take a banner with the Brazilian's name to every home and away game. Zico had a great streak at Udinese Calcio, scoring 59 goals in 73 games.
- Zico spent the maximum of his playing days with Brazilian club Flamengo, serving them for 16 years in two time periods: 1971 to 1983 and from 1985 to 1989 after he left Udinese Calcio.
- Zico also pitched for a manager's role in England as he lobbied for Kevin Keegan's role in Newcastle after his departure. Zico was reportedly offered the role of Alex Ferguson's assistant at Manchester United.
- Zico became Brazil's first sports minister in 1990, six years before Pelé was appointed for the same role. After just 13 months, a disgusted Zico quit the post when politicians linked to football authorities intentionally delayed a parliamentary vote on his project to modernize Brazilian football.
- Zico spent the last three years of his playing career with the Japanese club Kashima Antlers, from 1991 to 1994. Zico is hailed as 'God' by his Japanese fans, and thanks to his efforts, the standard of Japanese football grew by leaps and bounds.

- Zico was always good-natured and relished challenges in life. In 1994, he was invited to play beach soccer and accepted. He scored 12 goals and helped his team win the Beach Soccer World Cup in 1995.
- After his retirement, Zico was the technical director of the Kashima Antlers. Zico also managed other teams like FC Goa of India and the Japanese national football team before coaching the Kashima Antlers again. He proved to be a great success as a manager just like he was as a player.
- Often called the 'White Pelé' in Brazil, Zico never won a World Cup for his country like many other greats like Puskás and Cruyff. But he has earned a name in the list of all-time greats in football. In 2000, he was behind only Pelé and Garrincha among Brazilians in the FIFA 'Player of the Century' vote.

Zidane

- Legendary French footballer of Algerian descent Zinedine Zidane was born on 23 June 1972 in Marseille, France. He began playing football in the rough streets of La Castellane. His talent was discovered in a youth club when he was 14.
- After three years in the Cannes Youth Division, Zidane made his professional debut for Cannes aged 17, scoring his first goal. In 1992, he was picked up by Bordeaux.
- There are two stories behind the origin of Zinedine Zidane's nickname Zizou. The first is a friend calling him Zizou after another skilled player of the same

Zinedine Zidane

name. The second is when some called him Zizi, which was changed to Zizou as Zizi was French slang for the male private organ.

- The 1998 World Cup was the highlight of Zidane's career. In the final against Brazil, he scored 2 of the 3 French goals and troubled the star-studded Brazilian side. Zidane was named the Man of the Match as France won the World Cup.
- Zidane received the Legion d'honneur from the French government, the highest French honour, after France won the 1998 World Cup.

- Zidane moved from Juventus to Real Madrid for a record-breaking transfer fee of $81 million in 2001. Zidane justified his signing by taking Madrid to new heights. But as a kid, Zidane's favourite team in Spain was Barcelona. Madrid fans won't like that!
- During his career, Zidane has received several accolades, including three FIFA World Player of the Year awards in 1998, 2000, and 2003. In 1998, he won the Ballon d'Or. Other titles include Serie A Footballer of the Year, Ligue 1 Player of the Year, and La Liga Best Foreign Player. In 2006, Zidane received the Golden Ball award.
- Zidane has also had his shares of cards on the pitch. He has received the most cards in the World Cup, being booked by referees six times. His infamous red card came in 2006 when he headbutted Italian player Marco Materazzi. Zidane has received the red card 16 times in his career.
- Zinedine Zidane is officially the first footballer to have broken the sound barrier with a football kick. In a poll conducted by *Le Journal du Dimanche*, a French newspaper, Zidane was voted the most popular French footballer of all time.
- The UEFA Golden Jubilee poll revealed how popular Zidane really was among football lovers. He was voted the Best European Footballer in UEFA for the past 50 years. That's high praise!
- In his time, Zidane was one of the highest-paid footballers apart from being one of the most talented in history. Sponsorships with major brands like Lego, Adidas, France Telecom, Audi, Orange, Christian Dior,

and Volvic have earned Zidane over $10 million in revenue.

- Real Madrid is one of the greatest clubs of Spain and Europe and has won the maximum number of Champions League trophies. Since its inception, there have been almost 47 coaches who have all raised the bar higher. However, Zidane was the first French coach of Real Madrid in its 110-year existence.
- Zinedine Zidane is the fourth Real Madrid coach who has also won the World Cup as a player. The other three coaches are Hector Scarone, who won it in 1930, Jupp Heynckes (1974), and Jorge Valdano, who was part of the 1986 World Cup–winning Argentine team.
- It wasn't an easy ride to become the coach of Real Madrid. In 2009, Zidane became the club's advisor. In 2011, he was appointed as the club's sporting director. In 2013–14, he served as the assistant coach to Carlo Ancelotti. Then, he coached Real Madrid's B team – Real Madrid Castilla.
- Zidane is held in high esteem even outside France. When he was invited to Bangladesh by the Nobel Peace Prize Winner Muhammad Yunus, the Bangladeshi government gave Zidane an official reception, and the love displayed for Zidane by Bangladeshis was overwhelming. He received the same love in Algeria, where his parents were born.
- The song 'Zinedine Zidane' released in June 2014 on YouTube became a smash hit. The song is performed by Vaudeville Smash, an Australian group from Coburg, Melbourne. The vocalist is Les Murray, famous as the voice of soccer for Australia.

- Zidane's fans would like to see him coach the French national team soon. That day may not be far off as Zidane has had a good stint as the assistant coach of the Belgian team that has performed well in recent times, except the World Cup, of course.
- Zidane was selected by Qatar as ambassador for their bid to host the 2022 World Cup. Despite controversies, Zidane was happy when Qatar won the bid as he felt that football was a sport meant to be enjoyed by the whole world.

Ronaldo Nazario

- Ronaldo Luís Nazário de Lima or the Brazilian Ronaldo was born on 18 September 1976. He was named O Fenômeno or 'the Phenomenon' and also given the nickname R9. Ronaldo is regarded as one of the greatest strikers of all time.
- Sadly, Ronaldo could never play for the club he idolized as a child. Ronaldo was a Flamengo fanatic during his local days in Rio de Janeiro. He could not go for a trial to Flamengo as it was on the opposite side of the city and an expensive affair. So, he played for the Corinthians instead.
- A 17-year-old Ronaldo was a substitute during the 1994 World Cup, which Brazil won, although he did not get a chance to play. From 1994 to 1999, Ronaldo played under the name Ronaldinho for Brazil, which means 'little Ronaldo'.
- The reason Ronaldo had to change his name was because there was already a Big Ronaldo in the

Ronaldo Nazário

Brazilian side when he arrived, and two same names would cause confusion. That's why Ronaldo Rodrigues de Jesus was called Ronaldo, and he was called Ronaldinho or little Ronaldo.

- Confusion reigned supreme when another Ronaldo joined the Brazilian team, named Ronaldo de Assis Moreira. Thankfully, Ronaldo Rodrigues de Jesus retired, and little Ronaldo was called Ronaldo again. The newest Ronaldo was called Ronaldinho, and he sensibly decided to retain this name to avoid further confusion.

- In 1996, a 20-year-old Ronaldo joined FC Barcelona from PSV Eindhoven for a world record fee of £19 million then. He scored 47 goals in 49 appearances for Barcelona, which is an amazing feat. Ronaldo helped Barcelona win the Spanish Cup and the UEFA Cup Winners Cup.
- When Ronaldo was just 21, he was awarded the FIFA Player of the Year award and the coveted Ballon d'Or prize in 1997. He still remains the youngest footballer to receive the Ballon d'Or. He has won the FIFA World Player of the Year thrice and the Ballon d'Or award twice in his career.
- The game that led to his nickname 'the Phenomenon' was the 1998 UEFA Cup final in Paris between Inter Milan and Lazio. The match was positioned as a battle between the great striker Ronaldo of Inter Milan versus the great defender Alessandro Nesta of Lazio.
- But it was a cakewalk for Ronaldo as Inter Milan beat Lazio 3–0 with Ronaldo scoring the final goal and getting the better of Nesta. After the game, Nesta confessed that it was the worst experience of his career and Ronaldo was simply unstoppable.
- Old Trafford witnessed some Ronaldo magic on 23 April 2003 when Real Madrid faced Manchester United in the Champions League quarter-finals. The Red Devils won the match 4–3 but did not progress to the semis on aggregate scoreline because of Ronaldo's stunning hat-trick.
- When Ronaldo was substituted after scoring the hat-trick as Madrid brought on a defender to secure the game, he received a standing ovation from the

Manchester United fans that shocked even Ronaldo. Ronaldo left the pitch hands over his head, applauding the fans back. David Beckham stated later that Ronaldo had obliterated them.

- Despite Ronaldo's World Cup triumph and superb performances at the club level at Inter Milan, FC Barcelona, Real Madrid, and AC Milan, he could never win the Champions League title. It was this failure that led to his being booed by the over-critical Madrid fans.
- Ronaldo scored 85 goals for Real Madrid in his three-year tenure. Yet, the Real supporters were critical because he couldn't win the Champions League and taunted Ronaldo about his weight and his failure. In 2006, a disgruntled Ronaldo left Madrid and moved to AC Milan.
- The two-time World Cup champion for Brazil was body shamed by the media and fans after his excessive weight gain in the last years of his career. This was insensitive as Ronaldo suffered from hypothyroidism, which he revealed later.
- To continue playing the game, Ronaldo had to take hormone injections prior to the match, which was banned by the regulatory board in football. So, he decided to call it a day and retired from professional football in 2011.
- Ronaldo was actively involved with football even after retirement and co-owned many football teams. He is the president of Segunda División club Real Valladolid and the owner of Brasileiro Série B club Cruzeiro. Ronaldo was appointed as a goodwill ambassador

by the United Nations to work for many charitable organizations.

- Ronaldo was the co-owner of racing team A1 Team Brazil with motorsport legend Emerson Fittipaldi. The Brazilian also has a sports marketing company called 9INE with his friend Anderson Silva. Ronaldo is a great poker player and became a member of Pokerstars SportsStar in 2013.

Ronaldinho

- Ronaldo de Assis Moreira was famously known as Ronaldinho Gaúcho or just Ronaldinho. The Brazilian attacking midfielder was a key member of the Brazilian side that won the World Cup in 2002. He was a part of the famous Brazilian attacking trio – 'The Three Rs' – with Ronaldo and Rivaldo.
- The nickname Ronaldinho first happened in the youth club matches, 'inho' meaning small. This was because he was always the smallest, as well as the youngest, player in these matches. The nickname stuck in the Brazilian team to avoid confusion with the other Ronaldo.
- Born on 21 March 1980 in the city of Porto Alegre, Ronaldinho was introduced early to football as his father and brother were footballers too. In fact, Ronaldinho's brother was given a house by a club trying to sign him. Sadly, Roberto stopped playing after an injury.
- Tragedy struck when Ronaldinho was just eight years old. His father had an accident in the swimming

Ronaldinho

pool of their new house, hit his head and drowned. Ronaldinho's footballing skills had surfaced during this time, and Roberto decided to manage his talented younger brother. His sister, Deisi, became his press coordinator later.

- During his early days, Ronaldinho was more interested in futsal and beach football, and this interest later mushroomed into a love for football. Ronaldinho's signature moves and tricks are thanks to his experiences and skills honed in futsal or indoor football. His ball control is so good because the game in futsal is faster.

- Ronaldinho has won two FIFA World Player of the Year awards and a Ballon d'Or. Considering the extent of the Barcelona–Real Madrid rivalry, he is only the second Barcelona player, after Diego Maradona in 1983, to receive a standing ovation from Real Madrid fans at the Santiago Bernabéu.
- In 2004, Pelé named Ronaldinho in the FIFA 100 list of the world's greatest living players. Ronaldinho was declared UEFA Club Footballer of the Year for the 2005–06 season and South American Footballer of the Year in 2013.
- The Nike ad featuring Ronaldinho smashing the crossbar with his new boots smashed the internet as well with a record one million views on YouTube in 2005, being the first video to do so. That speaks volumes about Ronaldinho's popularity.
- In January 2007, Ronaldinho became a Spanish citizen, and this move did not go down well with some of his Brazilian fans. But this move meant travelling and working in Spain without any restrictions and was a major step forward in his career.
- Ronaldinho's collection of fancy cars is right up there with an Audi Q7, a Hummer 2, and a $1.3 million Bugatti Veyron among the ones that he owns. Well, he's always loved speed.
- Ronaldinho has endorsed some of the biggest brands, like Nike, Pepsi, Coca-Cola, EA Sports, and Danone, to name a few. In 2006, he earned a staggering $19 million from endorsements alone. But he also lost a big $7,50,000 sponsorship deal with Coca-Cola. Well, you can't win them all!

Pelé, Ronaldo, Ronaldinho and Others | Brazil – Best FIFA World Cup Goals

- Ronaldinho breached a Coca-Cola sponsorship deal when he was photographed holding a Pepsi drink at a press conference. Pepsi was the sponsor of his then club Atlético Mineiro. Coca-Cola cancelled the deal within less than a year of signing because of a conflict of interest and a breach of contract.
- In 2011, Ronaldinho teamed up with the United Nations to educate people about AIDS. Two years later, Ronaldinho realized a business opportunity as he launched his brand of club-themed condoms called 'Sex Free'. Free Kick would have been an apt name considering it's Ronaldinho.

Messi

- Luis Lionel Andres Messi was born in Rosario, Argentina on 24 June 1987 and quickly earned a reputation as a prodigy in football. A 13-year-old Messi joined FC Barcelona's Youth Academy in 2000.

Lionel Messi

Three years later, he made his Barcelona debut to slowly become one of the greatest players of his era.

- When Messi was 11 years old, he suffered from growth hormone deficiency that negatively impacted his normal growth rate. The medical costs were steep, at $900 per month, which his parents could not afford.
- His father's medical insurance covered only two years of Messi's treatment. A Buenos Aires club wanted to sign Messi but could not afford his treatment. So, a

trial was arranged with Barcelona with the help of Messi's Catalonian relatives in September 2000.

- The first team director of Barcelona was so impressed with the young Messi that he wanted to sign him on the spot before anyone else could do so. As there was no paper at hand, Messi's first contract was quickly scribbled on a paper napkin.
- Messi's father stayed back with him in Barcelona while his mother flew back to Argentina. During his initial years, Messi suffered from homesickness and missed Argentina. Slowly, he got used to Spain and made it his second home.
- Strangely, in his stint with the Barcelona youth team, Messi could not play for the first year because he was a foreign player. He was a shy boy who did not talk much, and his teammates initially thought that he was mute. But Messi made the ball talk!
- The former manager of Arsenal, Arsène Wenger, tried his best to sign Messi at a young age when he was at Barcelona's La Masia Academy, realizing his phenomenal talent. This was right after Arsenal had signed Cesc Fàbregas. But Messi refused the offer from Arsenal.
- 17-year-old Messi made his Barcelona debut against RCD Espanyol. Messi became the third-youngest player to start for Barcelona and the youngest-ever player to score a goal for the Catalonian club.
- Messi signed his first contract as a senior team player for Barcelona on his 18th birthday. It was his best birthday gift! The contract had a buy-out clause of €150 million and extended until 2010.

- Messi's incredible performance against Italian club Juventus impressed everyone, including Fabio Capello, the then-Juventus coach. He requested his club to loan Messi, which was refused. Inter Milan then offered to buy Messi and were willing to pay his €150 million release clause and triple his wages too. But Messi refused.
- As Messi spent seven years of his professional career in Spain, he could have opted to play for Spain. The Royal Spanish Football Federation asked Messi to join the Spanish football team, but he refused. Messi chose to play for the country of his birth and became Argentina's all-time top goal scorer.
- Messi's idol in his growing-up years was fellow Argentina and former Valencia and Real Zaragoza play-maker Pablo Aimar. The two faced each other in La Liga on many occasions. On a special night in 2004, Aimar gave his jersey to a thrilled Messi.
- Pablo Aimar was also part of Argentina's 2022 World Cup team that Messi captained to glory. Aimar played a pivotal role in this triumph as he was the assistant manager to head coach Lionel Scaloni.
- In the 2006 World Cup, Messi became the youngest-ever Argentinian player to play in a World Cup. He was 18 years, 11 months and 23 days old. In his debut match, Messi became the sixth youngest player to score in the FIFA World Cup.
- Messi made his international debut for Argentina as a 17-year-old on 17 August 2005 in a friendly against Hungary. Messi was introduced as a substitute in the second half at the Puskás Arena in Budapest in the

64th minute. But he was sent off less than a minute later.

- Messi has steered Barcelona to 10 La Liga titles, 4 Champions League titles and has also led Argentina to wins in the Copa America 2021 and the 2022 FIFA World Cup. He has received the Ballon d'Or trophy a record seven times along with several individual awards.
- Messi missed the 2006 UEFA Champions League final because of injury. Barcelona beat Arsenal in Paris even with Messi absent. The passionate Messi was so disappointed at missing the finals that he did not celebrate that Champions League victory. This was a rash decision he regretted later.
- On 1 May 2007, a 19-year-old Messi scored his first hat-trick for Barcelona, and that too against arch-rivals Real Madrid at Camp Nou. He received ample help from colleague and Brazilian legend Ronaldinho. The match ended in a 3–3 draw though.
- After his first training session at Barcelona, Ronaldinho realized what a great player Messi was. He told his teammates then and there that Messi would become the greatest player in the world and mentored him. The relationship between the two legends was special, and Ronaldinho called Messi his 'little brother'.
- When he was 20 years old, Messi was given the nickname of 'Messiah' by the Spanish media because of his superlative performances in La Liga. After Ronaldinho left Barcelona in 2008, Messi inherited the iconic number 10 shirt and did justice to it.

- Messi is undoubtedly Barcelona's most decorated player and one of the best ever. The 35 major trophies he has won with Barca bear testimony to this fact. These include 10 La Liga crowns, 7 Copa del Rey triumphs, 4 Champions League wins, 3 FIFA Club World Cup victories, 3 UEFA Super Cup, and 8 Supercopa de España wins.
- Messi is also the Spanish league's greatest goal scorer, having scored a stunning 474 goals in La Liga. In 2014, he beat Telmo Zarra's record when he scored his 252nd La Liga goal. No one has been able to catch up with Messi after that.
- Once, during a match in the Copa Catalunya, Messi had to play with a plastic protector mask to cover his broken cheekbone. But after a few minutes, Messi took off the mask as it was bothersome to play with and scored 2 goals in 10 minutes before he was substituted as a safety measure.
- We are accustomed to seeing Messi pointing towards the sky with both hands after scoring a goal. This is Messi's tribute to his grandmother, Celia, who kindled Messi's interest in the sport and helped him take his first steps with a football. Sadly, Celia died in 1998 and could not witness her grandson's success.
- Messi also replicated the two famous Diego Maradona goals against England in a span of three weeks. In the Copa Del Rey semi-final, he scored a goal similar to the 'Goal of the Century'. He scored a goal similar to the 'Hand of God' goal against Espanyol in a league match.

- Thanks largely to Messi, Barcelona achieved the first-ever treble in Spanish football history. Barcelona became the Champions of Europe after beating Manchester United 2–0 in the final, where Messi scored with a header.
- Barcelona completed their sextuple in 2009 after winning the Champions League, La Liga, Spanish Cup, Club World Cup, UEFA Super Cup, and the Copa del Rey. A 22-year-old Messi won his first Ballon d'Or and the FIFA World Player of the Year award because of these incredible achievements.
- In the 2010 FIFA World Cup, Messi wore Argentina's captain armband for the first time against Greece. But a major trophy was elusive for Messi for a long time with Argentina till the storm arrived. Messi led Argentina to victories in the Copa America and the FIFA World Cup in the span of a year in 2022.
- Famous coach José Mourinho was in for a rude shock during his first match in charge of Real Madrid that faced Barcelona in an El Clásico encounter. Messi shone in Barcelona's 5–0 drubbing of Real Madrid in that game.
- Messi became the top scorer in a single season in the history of European club football when he scored 73 goals for Barcelona in all competitions. Messi beat German Gerd Müller's record of 67 goals in the 1972–73 Bundesliga season.
- Messi displayed his humility and respect for the German legend when he sent Gerd Müller his number 10 Barcelona T-shirt signed 'with respect and admiration' after breaking Müller's 40-year-old record.

- Barcelona had a poor run of form during Messi's injury in 2013. The term 'Messidependencia' was created to highlight just how important Messi was for Barça.
- But Messi returned in style, scoring a hat-trick against Real Madrid in the second half of the 2013–14 season. This broke Real Madrid legend Di Stéfano's record of 18 goals and made Messi the top scorer in all El Clásicos.
- Speaking of hat-tricks, Messi scored his fastest hat-trick in 11 minutes against Rayo Vallecano on 8 March 2015. This was his 32nd hat-trick for Barcelona, a record in Spanish football. He is currently Barcelona's all-time top-scorer from free kicks too.
- On 19 May 2014, Messi signed a new contract with Barcelona, which increased his salary to €36 million before taxes, the highest salary ever in football. Messidependencia? You bet!
- Messi is famous off the pitch for his philanthropic work. The Leo Messi Foundation established by him improves the lives of children in need worldwide. His

Lionel Messi | 10 Great Goals | FIFA

several charitable initiatives include a special project to build a children's hospital in his hometown Rosario in Argentina.

Cristiano Ronaldo

- Cristiano Ronaldo was born and raised in Madeira and is Portugal's most famous personality around the world today. He has a staggering 446 million followers on Instagram, which vouches for his popularity. His fans call him CR7 because of his initials and jersey number just like Messi is called LM10.
- Cristiano Ronaldo is a working-class hero born to a poor Portuguese family as the fourth and youngest child. His mother was a cook, and his father was a gardener. His father was an alcoholic who died in 2005 from liver failure. Ronaldo's journey was no easy road.
- In her book *Mãe Coragem* ('Mother Courage'), Ronaldo's mother, Dolores Aveiro, reveals how she contemplated terminating her pregnancy when she was pregnant with Cristiano because of her family's extreme poverty and her husband's alcohol addiction. As football fans, all we can say is thank you for doing the sensible thing!
- Apart from alcohol, Cristiano Ronaldo's dad also liked the movies, and Ronald Reagan (of all people) was his favourite actor before Reagan decided to become the president of the United States. So, Ronaldo was named after Ronald Reagan because his parents thought the name sounded 'strong'.

Cristiano Ronaldo

- When he was growing up, Ronaldo's nickname was 'cry baby'. He was called this by family and friends as the little striker would cry when he passed the ball and his friends were unable to score a goal. Although he doesn't do that now, he still reacts pretty strongly when the same occurs.
- For someone like Cristiano Ronaldo, nicknames were the obvious choice to address him. His actual name is Cristiano Ronaldo dos Santos Aveiro.

- CR7 was also nicknamed 'little bee' as a child, not because of his buzzing abilities but because of his exceptional speed on the field. We have all seen that, haven't we? Sadly, he is one of the legends of the game not to have won the World Cup. In fact, his country, Portugal, has never won.
- Speaking of speed, Ronaldo reached an astonishing 32.51 km/h while playing for Manchester United in a match against West Ham in September 2021. He became the fastest footballer in any game.
- When he was 14, Ronaldo was extremely popular with his schoolmates. The popularity went to his head, and once, he flung a chair towards a teacher and was lucky not to be expelled from school. His mother advised him to focus on football instead of silly things, and he did just that.
- Ronaldo had heart surgery when he was 15 years old. He was diagnosed with tachycardia, causing a rapid heartbeat of over 100 times a minute, which can lead to stroke or heart failure. After the surgery, Ronaldo was back playing football only after a few days.
- Ronaldo attributes his success to his friend Albert Fantrau. In his younger years, Albert was admitted to a football academy but turned the offer down, and Ronaldo was taken in his place. When Ronaldo asked Alfred why he refused the position, he replied, 'You're better than me.'
- Controversy erupted in 2005 when Cristiano Ronaldo was arrested over the alleged rape of two women at a London hotel. He denied the charge, and the case was dropped by Scotland Yard due to lack of evidence. In

2009 in Las Vegas, he was accused of rape again, while he claimed that it was consensual and was eventually acquitted.

- Cristiano Ronaldo sued the *Daily Telegraph* in 2008 after its report stated that the player had risked his injured ankle by partying in a Hollywood nightclub with models. The paper admitted the report was fabricated and offered Ronaldo a libel payout that he accepted in 2010.
- Ronaldo also sued the *Sun* and accepted damages because it claimed that he had broken Manchester United's rules by using a phone during training. The large-hearted Ronaldo donated the damages he earned to a charity in Madeira.
- In 2009, Real Madrid insured Cristiano Ronaldo's legs for over €100 million. But this is not the most expensive body part insurance in football. Lionel Messi's left foot is insured at €750 million.
- Much as CR7 is loved for his footballing skills and accomplishments, he also has his share of critics and haters. Many do not like the legend, perceiving him as arrogant and aloof. In 2011, Ronaldo increased this number further when he stated that some people didn't like him because he was too handsome, rich and more talented than anyone else.
- In December 2012, Cristiano Ronaldo joined FIFA 11 For Health Foundation, the objective of which is to create awareness amongst children for conditions like HIV, obesity, malaria, and drug addiction.
- The CR7 Museum is a special museum that celebrates the life and achievements of Cristiano Ronaldo. It was

founded in 2013 in his birthplace in Funchal, Madeira. The unique museum features CR7's photos, trophies, medals and footballs he played with.

- One can actually study the sociology of Cristiano Ronaldo at Canada's University of British Columbia Okanagan. In 2015, this sociology fourth-year course about Cristiano Ronaldo was introduced by UBC Okanagan Associate Professor Luís L.M. Aguiar. He declared, 'Ronaldo's social and cultural appeal transcends football, making him an interesting study.'
- In 2015, Cristiano Ronaldo was declared the world's highest-paid player. In 2014, his total earnings from salaries, bonuses, endorsements and other incomes amounted to $73 million. In 2017, this had gone up to a staggering $93 million.
- Ronaldo shared a great relationship with his Manchester United manager Sir Alex Ferguson. It was Sir Alex who insisted that Ronaldo wear jersey number 7, to emulate his great predecessors at Manchester United who wore 7, like Eric Cantona, George Best, and David Beckham. Little did he know then that a brand named CR7 would be created.
- Ronaldo's mother was instrumental in his Real Madrid move as she loves Madrid. When Ronaldo moved to Real Madrid, he was greeted by 80,000 fans at the Santiago Bernabéu Stadium. The previous record holder was Diego Maradona, who was greeted by 75,000 fans in his first match in 1984.
- Ronaldo's rags-to-riches story is like a fairy tale. The transition from a slum dweller to becoming the richest

footballer in the world is no small feat. According to *Forbes*, Ronaldo is also the first footballer to become a billionaire. It's certainly well-deserved.

- Ronaldo signed a lifetime endorsement deal with Nike worth $1 billion, becoming the third sportsman to do so after LeBron James and Michael Jordan. *Forbes* reported that Ronaldo's mere social media presence in 2016 earned Nike $474 million thanks to just 329 posts by Ronaldo.
- CR7 had 240 million followers across all platforms in 2016 when he signed the lifetime deal with Nike. Today, just his Instagram followers are to the tune of 395 million and growing steadily, making him the most followed person on Instagram.
- 2016 was certainly a special year for CR7. Cupid struck Ronaldo at a Gucci store in Madrid of all places when he met his partner Georgina Rodriguez while she was working as a shop assistant there. She was 22 and Ronaldo was 31 then. The couple has been together for six years and has five lovely children.
- Ronaldo owns at least eight homes and is currently on the verge of building a retirement mansion even though he hasn't retired yet. His property is valued at over $54 million, and he possesses several luxury cars like a limited edition $10.7 million Bugatti Centodieci. Ronaldo lives the life of the 1 per cent super-rich of the global population.
- CR7 has scored 900 career goals and is still going strong. He is already the highest-ever goal scorer in men's soccer history. Messi is still 62 goals away

Cristiano Ronaldo | Great Last-Minute Goals

from CR7. He might just catch up, being three years younger. But that's a different story.

- Ronaldo's famous jump utilized mainly to head the ball inside the opponent's goal is a modern mystery of nature. CR7 generates five times the power of a cheetah in full flight when he makes this jump. This ensures that he reaches 44 cm in the air from a standing start and 78 cm with a run-up.
- Cristiano Ronaldo does not have a single tattoo on his body, and he has vowed to never get tattoos. This is because he donates blood regularly and is not willing to wait months after a tattoo is done to be able to do so. He's also a registered bone marrow donor.
- There's also a four-star hotel named the Pestana CR7 Funchal right above the museum built in partnership between Ronaldo and the Pestana Group. One wonders why CR7 built a four-star hotel and not something bigger though.

- Ronaldo has had brands chasing him for endorsement deals throughout his football career. He has endorsed numerous brands like Coca-Cola, Armani jeans and underwear, Nike, Konami, Motorola, KFC, Jacob & Co., Fly Emirates, Castrol, Herbalife, and more.
- Love him or hate him, there is no denying that Cristiano Ronaldo is a true legend of the game and that too, with a golden heart. He sold his golden boot in the past to donate the money to fund schools in Gaza for needy children.

Mbappé

- French superstar Kylian Mbappé plays for PSG and the French national team and was born in 1998. In just a short span of time, he has become a legend of the game. Mbappé started his career with Monaco, helping them win the Ligue 1 title win in the 2016–17 season.
- Mbappé scored 11 goals when Monaco won the Ligue 1, and this impressive performance earned him a place in the French national team in 2017. Mbappé has scored 253 goals in 363 games for club and country, and this tally outshines both Messi and Ronaldo's haul when they were his age.
- Mbappé was born in Bondy, France, to a family of sportspersons. His father, Wilfried Mbappé, was a football coach who became his agent later. Mbappé's mother, Fayza Lamari, had represented France in handball. Mbappé credits his father as his biggest inspiration.

Kylian Mbappé

- When Mbappé was five years old, he used to sit in with his father during his tactical discussions as a youth coach with the local club AS Bondy. That led to his absorbing tactical information at an impressionable age.
- Mbappé was the youngest player ever to join AS Monaco at 14, although he started playing for the club at 16. The then manager of Monaco, Thierry Henry, had been the youngest player of Monaco till Mbappé arrived.

- At 17, Mbappé became the youngest scorer for Monaco, breaking another Thierry Henry record. Mbappé was famously addressed in his hometown as 'the next Thierry Henry' when he was growing up. This feeling was echoed by Arsène Wenger in 2017 who tried to recruit Mbappé for Arsenal.
- Although Kylian Mbappé didn't join Arsenal, he almost joined Chelsea in 2012. Mbappé gave a trial at Chelsea, who wanted another trial as they were not satisfied. Mbappé's mother rejected the offer, saying famously, 'Either they sign him now, or within five years they'll have to offer €50 million to tie him down.'
- Although Mbappé decided to play for France, he could have also opted to play for two more countries. He could have represented either Algeria or Cameroon if he chose to. Mbappé's mother hails from Algeria, and his father was born in Cameroon.
- Mbappé's move from Monaco to PSG made him one of the most expensive teenage footballers ever. As a 20-year-old, he was instrumental in France winning the 2018 FIFA World Cup for the second time in their history. He became the youngest French player to win the World Cup.
- Mbappé scored 4 goals in the 2018 FIFA World Cup and was awarded the tournament's Best Young Player award. Mbappé has also won the Ligue 1 Player of the Year award thrice in a row (2018–19, 2020–21, 2021–22). He could have won it a fourth time, but the trophy wasn't awarded during the pandemic.
- Mbappé's favourite thing as a child was a pair of sneakers. His first pair was the Nike Air Maxes, and

he would beg his mother to buy him new sneakers and cry his heart out when she wouldn't. Today, Nike has a special section on their website called 'BOUTIQUE DE MBAPPÉ' featuring Mbappé's choice in footwear.

- The first football boots that Mbappé possessed were Nike Vapors. These football boots were so coveted that his teammates would ask Mbappé if they could borrow them when he wasn't playing. The requests were always declined.
- Mbappé's childhood idol is the mercurial Portuguese Cristiano Ronaldo, and his room was full of CR7's posters. He is still a big fan. But who would have ever thought that the fan would outshine the idol on football's biggest stage so soon.
- 23-year-old Mbappé became the youngest player to score a hat-trick in a World Cup final when he slammed 3 goals past Argentina in the final of the 2022 World Cup. France were denied their second back-to-back title after Argentina beat them on penalties.
- Mbappé won the Golden Boot in the 2002 World Cup, scoring 8 goals in the tournament. He is sixth on the list of France's all-time goal scorers with 36 goals to his credit, just one behind Karim Benzema.
- Mbappé has scored 12 World Cup goals in the 14 matches he has played. He is level with Brazilian legend Pelé and is sixth currently on the list of all-time goal scorers. He is also the second footballer to hit the net in successive World Cup finals after Brazilian Vavá.
- Mbappé has had a strong presence in the Champions League as well. He made his debut in 2016–17, and in

51 appearances, he has been involved in 54 Champions League goals. That includes 31 goals and 20 assists.

- Mbappé donated all his earnings from the FIFA World Cup 2018 in Russia to a children's charity named Premiers de cordée. This was close to half a million US dollars. Mbappé's reasoning was that he felt he should not be paid to represent France.
- Mbappé certainly thinks he should be paid for endorsements, though. He signed a 10-year deal with Nike in 2019, believed to be worth £140 million plus bonuses. He has endorsed Nike since 2015, but after the 2018 World Cup, there was a great bidding war for Mbappé among Adidas, Puma, and Nike.
- The donation of his earnings to charity after the World Cup win was not a one-off thing for Mbappé. He has always been actively involved in charitable work and has his own charity called the Kylian Mbappé Foundation, which helps underprivileged children in France and Africa by providing education and sports opportunities.
- Mbappé is one of the fastest movers on the football pitch. During a game in 2019, Mbappé clocked 23.61 miles per hour – .25 miles per hour faster than Usain Bolt when he won the 100 m race in 2009. However, Bolt bettered this in Berlin, clocking 27.8 miles per hour. But Bolt doesn't have to run with a football, does he?
- When Mbappé was 23 years old, he found a place on the *Forbes* list of the world's highest-paid football players. His expected annual earnings were to the tune of a record $128 million.

- Like many young footballers, Mbappé is also a car fanatic. He possesses a fleet of luxurious cars like the Ferrari 488 Pista and the Mercedes V Class. He lives in the 16th arrondissement in a luxurious 600-square-meter apartment with a view of the Eiffel Tower.
- Mbappé is a social media sensation with almost 100 million followers on Instagram and 17 million followers on Facebook. In fact, he has more Instagram followers than French President Macron.

Kylian Mbappé | FIFA World Cup Goals

7

MASTERS OF THE GAME: FOOTBALL COACHES

- Helmut Schön was the highly successful coach of the West German football team. He led his team to the World Cup final in 1966 and 1974, as well as the semi-final in 1970. The 1978 World Cup was the only failure in his resume as defending champions.
- Only three coaches/managers have won the World Cup both as a coach and a player. Brazilian Mário Zagallo won as a player in 1958 and 1962 and as a coach in 1970. German Franz Beckenbauer won as a player in 1974 and as a coach in 1990. Didier Deschamps was a member of the French team in 1998 and was the victorious coach in 2018.
- Only six coaches have managed to lead their teams to the final of the World Cup twice. They are Victor Pozzo, Helmut Schön, Mário Zagallo, Franz Beckenbauer, Carlos Bilardo, and Didier Deschamps. But only Pozzo won the World Cup twice in 1934 and 1938 with Italy.

- Strangely, no team with a foreign coach has ever won the FIFA World Cup. The winning coaches have all been of the same nationality as the team.
- Franz Beckenbauer's unique coaching style was all about enjoying the game and making sure that one didn't concede a goal. Under his managership, Olympique de Marseille won the Ligue 1 title in the 1990–91 season. He also led Bayern Munich to a win in the Bundesliga in 1993–94 and the UEFA Cup in 1995–96.
- Sir Matt Busby managed to ensure that Manchester United became league champions twice: the early '50s and the late '60s. The Red Devils were called the Busby Babes then because of the young players that Busby coached, like Bobby Charlton and Duncan Edwards.
- Unfortunately, eight footballers of the Busby Babes died in the Munich air tragedy of 1958 when their aircraft crashed during take-off. A determined Sir Matt Busby built a brand-new team that won 2 more First division titles. Busby had already won 3 for Manchester United before this, plus a European Cup.
- Fabio Capello managed Milan with great flourish in the early '90s so that they won 58 Serie A games in a row. Earlier, he was an exponent of the typical Italian defensive style, but later, he struck a balance with a characteristic offensive style.
- Fabio Capello was a tough boss. After managing various clubs like Milan, Real Madrid, Roma, and Juventus, he took charge of the English national football team and transformed their play. He developed a new style

of play where the Three Lions focused on passes and touches.

- Johan Cruyff implemented the tiki-taka strategy as manager to take Barcelona to new heights. The strategy had two key elements: short and quick passes with players moving around. Spain's World Cup–winning team used the tiki-taka strategy to great effect.
- The fact that Sir Alex Ferguson managed Manchester for as long as 25 years speaks volumes about his abilities. He is the most successful coach in English football history with a record 19 league titles, 2 UEFA Champions Leagues, and a FIFA Club World Cup. He has shaped individual talents like Eric Cantona, Wayne Rooney, and Roy Keane.
- Under manager Pep Guardiola, Barcelona has won more titles than any other manager. He received the

Pep Guardiola

FIFA Ballon d'Or as Best Coach in 2011. When he joined the team in 2008, Pep sold or loaned established players like Deco, Ronaldinho, and Samuel Eto'o to build a new team from the players at La Masia.

- Austrian coach Ernst Happel won league titles in as many as four European countries in a remarkable coaching career. Happel won in the Netherlands, Belgium, Germany, and Austria. Happel's signature move was his attacking strategy and to pressure the ball and smother the rivals. Happel also took the Dutch national team to the 1978 World Cup final.
- Helenio Herrera was nicknamed the 'Wizard' for his coaching abilities. He won 7 league titles with Atlético de Madrid, Barcelona, and Inter Milan. Herrera was one of the first managers who laid stress on proper fitness and diet for his footballers. In Barcelona, he used the wingers as inside forwards to make the team more attacking.
- Dutch manager Guus Hiddink has coached teams like PSV Eindhoven, Valencia, Real Madrid, and Chelsea, and the Dutch, South Korean and Russian national teams. Hiddink's USP is his ability to transform his defensive midfielders into attacking midfielders in the classic 4–4–2 formation.
- Guus Hiddink absolutely demands creative play from all his players and wants them to have an attacking mindset instead of a defensive one. He also prefers to rely on the entire team rather than a few stars. His tough achievements include taking the Aussies to the Round of 16 in the World Cup, making Russia qualify for the 2008 Euro, and winning 10 titles for his clubs.

- German manager Ottmar Hitzfeld helped Aarau win the Swiss league and repeated the same feat with Grasshopper in 1989 and 1990. Borussia Dortmund won the Bundesliga title after 30 years under Hitzfeld in 1994–95 and again in 1995–96. They also won the 1996–97 UEFA Champions League.
- Ottmar Hitzfeld was hired by Bayern Munich, whom he helped win a UEFA Champions League trophy, as well as 5 Bundesliga titles. Since 2008, Hitzfeld has built the Swiss team into a formidable force in world football, using his signature style of faster speed and tempo, fast touches and closing lines.
- Marcello Lippi coached Italy to victory in the 2006 World Cup using a simple mantra: the team must be united. Lippi firmly believed that a team couldn't succeed without possessing a strong mentality and team effort even if it had stars playing for it.
- Understandably, Marcello Lippi is the only manager to win both the World Cup and the Champions League titles. Before helming the affairs of the Italian national team, Lippi managed several clubs like Pontedera, Siena, Pistoiese, Carrarese, Cesena, Lucchese, Atalanta, Napoli, Juventus, and Inter Milan.
- Dutchman Rinus Michels is an important manager in the coaching manual as he was the inventor of 'total football' and influenced legends like Johan Cruyff. He managed the legendary Dutch team that lost to West Germany at the 1974 World Cup.
- José Mourinho is a dynamic coach in world football and has proved his worth managing clubs like Real Madrid, Chelsea, Benfica, Porto, União de Leiria, and

Inter Milan. His compact style of play resulted in a nine-year undefeated home run for Real Madrid in 150 games.

- Spaniard Miguel Muñoz cemented Real Madrid's position as one of the strongest teams in Europe. As their manager, he won the La Liga 9 times, failing to win in only two seasons in 1965–66 and 1969–70. He was the longest-serving coach of Real Madrid, spending 16 years with the club. He has coached some of the absolute legends including Alfredo Di Stéfano and Ferenc Puskás.
- Bob Paisley was the most successful coach in Liverpool's history. He managed Liverpool from 1974 to 1983 and won at least 1 title in eight of the nine seasons with the club. These titles included 6 First Division championships, 3 European Cups, and 5 FA Charity Shields.
- Italian manager Nereo Rocco invented the Catenaccio system, based on an efficient defensive line. The only task that this defensive line had was to prevent goals. Rocco led Triestina to the second place in Serie A, the best result the club has ever had, and the Catenaccio strategy became famous all over Europe.
- Nereo Rocco was hired by Milan, who were impressed by his defensive abilities. He moved on to the bigger club in Serie A and met their expectations, helping them win 2 European Cup titles in 1963 and 1969.
- Brazilian manager Luiz Felipe Scolari has managed an astonishing 17 teams in his evergreen career, including impressive names like Portugal, Brazil, Chelsea,

Palmeiras, and Cruzeiro. Scolari loves to experiment, and his favourite positions on the pitch are 4–3–2–1, 3–4–1–2 and 4–3–3.

- In Scolari's footballing strategy, the midfielders play a vital role in offence, making speedy runs through the centre of the field. The wingers also play an important role as he switches them periodically to transform them to execute diverse roles and set the pace of the game according to the situation.
- Giovanni Trapattoni followed Ernst Heppel's example when he won the league title as manager in four different countries: Austria, Germany, Italy, and Portugal. With his disciplined defensive strategy, Trapattoni tasted success in his stints for clubs like Milan, Juventus, Inter Milan, Bayern Munich, Benfica, and Salzburg.
- Arsène Wenger took over the reins of Arsenal in 1996 and won the club 3 Premier League titles, 4 FA Cups, and 4 Community Shields. Rather than buying high-profile players like other managers, Wenger focused on training youngsters to hone their skills. Wenger won 57 per cent of the games as manager in his 16 years with the Gunners.

8

AFRICAN AND INDIAN FOOTBALL

African Football

- The footballing rivalry between Nigeria and Ghana is legendary and the oldest rivalry in West Africa, with both nations trying hard to prove that they are better. Both these teams have played each other the maximum times among African teams – 49 times. The first match was played on 16 October 1950.
- One of the most famous and prestigious football tournaments in Africa is the Africa Cup of Nations. The tournament was first held in 1957 and has been held every two years since then. It is the oldest continental football championship.
- The Egyptian national team has won the Africa Cup of Nations more than any other African team. Egypt has won the tournament a record 7 times.
- Nigerian footballer Nwankwo Kanu is considered one of the greatest African footbailers. He has won the

African Footballer of the Year award twice, in 1996 and 1999.

- Cameroon star player Samuel Eto'o is the highest overall goal scorer in the Africa Cup of Nations. He has scored 18 goals in 6 tournaments between 2000 and 2010.
- Mali made one of the strongest comebacks in football history in a match against Senegal in 2004. Mali was trailing 4–0 at half-time. But in a dramatic and stunning turnaround in the second half, Mali pumped in 4 goals to secure a 4–4 draw.
- The Ghanaian national team is also called the Black Stars and found great success in international football. In 2010, they stormed into the quarter-finals of the World Cup and have also won the Africa Cup of Nations 4 times.
- The Algerian national football team was once considered a minnow in African football but has made remarkable progress in recent times to change that perception. At the 2014 World Cup, they managed to reach the Round of 16 and also lifted the Africa Cup of Nations in 2019.
- Morocco became the first African team to reach the semi-finals of the World Cup. The Atlas Lions achieved this feat in the Qatar 2022 World Cup. But fourteen players in the team were born outside Morocco.

Indian Football

- English soldiers first introduced football in India during the colonial period in the mid-19th century. The first football games in the country were played by British soldiers stationed in various army units across India.

- The first football club in India was Calcutta FC, which was established in 1872. Initially, the club was founded to field a cricket side in the 1840s by British lovers of the game. Later, the football team was also added.
- Gostha Pal was the first captain of the Indian national team and played during the 1920s and 1930s. This central defender was nicknamed 'the Chinese Wall' for his abilities as a central defender and spent most of his club career with Mohun Bagan. In 1962, he became the first Indian footballer to be honoured with the Padma Shri.
- Once, Mohun Bagan played a match against Calcutta FC, an all-English team. To protest the biased decisions the referee made in favour of the Englishmen, Gostha Pal ordered his players to lie down on the field. This was an iconic moment in Indian football.
- The partition of Bengal and the creation of Bangladesh caused the displacement of many Hindu Bengalis to India, who were termed refugees and labelled as 'Bangaals'. The original Bengali inhabitants were called 'Ghotis', and these two communities were responsible for the creation of the great Kolkata derby.
- The refugee Bangaals faced a lot of discrimination from the prosperous Ghotis for their culture, language, and habits. The two communities did not see eye to eye. Football was no different as Jorabagan Club often dropped two Bangaal players, Sailesh Bose and Ramesh Chandra Sen, from their playing eleven because of this discrimination.

- The discrimination against the two players from East Bengal irked a senior official in the management of the Jorabagan team. Suresh Chandra Chaudhury was also a Bangaal and decided to form a new football club with Bose and Sen and other Bangaal players. East Bengal Club was formed in North Calcutta on 1 August 1920.
- One of the legendary club rivalries in world football in terms of both popularity and social involvement is the Kolkata derby between East Bengal and Mohun Bagan, which began in 1920. Derby matches are mostly born because of racial, religious or political conflicts, and the Indian El Clásico is no different.
- The first time the Indian football team played a match, albeit unofficially, was in 1924. The team featured a mixed bag of local and British footballers who toured various countries to play friendly football games. The first officially recorded game was played in September 1938 against Australia, which India lost 5–3.
- Although India has never played in the FIFA World Cup, it has played 4 Olympic football tournaments, beginning with the London Olympics in 1948. India has won the South Asian Football Federation championship 8 times. 1951 to 1962 is considered the golden era in Indian football.
- In the 1948 London Olympics, the Indian football team lost 2–1 to France. The Indian team failed to convert 2 penalties in the match, missing a golden chance to win. India put up their best show at the 1956 Olympics when they finished fourth.

Sunil Chhetri

- The biggest margin of victories by the Indian football team in their history was when they drubbed Australia 7–1 on 12 December 1956 and humiliated Cambodia 6–0 on 17 August 2007. India suffered their biggest defeat at the hands of the former Soviet Union, losing 11–1 on 16 September 1955.
- Sunil Chhetri has earned the most caps among Indian footballers. The 37-year-old has made a record 125 appearances for the Blue Tigers since making his debut for India in 2005. Chhetri has also scored the maximum goals for India – a record 80 goals so far!
- The Premier League in India is known as the Indian Super League or the ISL. Many foreign footballers play in the ISL, and Atlético de Kolkata is the most successful Indian football club in the ISL.

- The Durand Cup is a local football competition played annually in India. It began in 1888 and is the oldest tournament in Asia. The Durand Cup is also the third-oldest Cup in the world, only after the English FA Cup and the Scottish Cup.
- India managed to qualify for the 1950 FIFA World Cup, but the All India Football Federation (AIFF) couldn't afford the travelling costs and other expenses. The second reason for non-participation was FIFA imposing a rule that banned teams from playing barefoot. The Indian team used to play barefoot then.
- Under the watchful eyes of the legendary Syed Abdul Rahim, India emerged as the best Asian team. Popularly known as Rahim Saab, he was the player, coach and manager of the Indian football team.
- Salgaocar Football Club of Goa has over 60 years of history dating to the pre-Liberation era of Goa. Goa was liberated in 1961, and prior to that, Salgaocar comprised mostly European players with just a few Goan players. Legendary defender Menino Figueiredo began the trend of Goan footballers in the club followed by stars Brahmanand Sankhwalkar and Bruno Coutinho later.
- The 1990s saw the meteoric rise of a football club from Kerala called FC Kochin. Local stars I.M. Vijayan and Jo Paul Ancheri were roped in to create a star-studded team with Bengal goalkeeper Sumit Mukherjee, Carlton Chapman, and Raman Vijayan. The foreign stars comprised Ghanaians like goalkeeper Ali Abubakar, midfielder Mohammed Salisu and the

Nigerian midfielder trio of Saeed Akinsanya, Bernard Oparanozie, and Friday Elaho.

- FC Kochin is the first Indian professional football club. The successful club is based in Kochi, Kerala, and was formed in the late 1990s. But the fall of FC Kochin in 1998–99 was faster than the rise. Mohun Bagan poached big guns I.M. Vijayan and Ancheri, and East Bengal lured away Chapman and Raman Vijayan. With the departure of their local stars, FC Kochi's slump began.
- In 2001, Nagpur-based sports teacher Vijay Barse founded 'slum soccer', which is a unique and innovative concept. Not only did it make football a popular sport in the slum areas but also reduced the high crime rates there. Barse got this idea when he observed underprivileged children play with a makeshift football.
- India has hosted only one FIFA tournament, which it also participated in. The FIFA U-17 World Cup was held in 2017, and this was the 17th edition of the tournament. The attendance for this tournament was a record 13,47,133.

9

BIZARRE FOOTBALL TALES

The Goalkeeper Who Became an Overnight Sensation

Singapore's goalkeeper became a superstar in another country, creating some amazing football news. When China lost to South Korea 1–0 in Seoul, Chinese hopes of reaching the third stage of the Asian qualifiers for the 2026 World Cup were crushed. The 2026 FIFA World Cup will be jointly hosted by the US, Canada, and Mexico. China's fate depended on another qualifying match to be played between Thailand and Singapore. Thailand needed to beat Singapore by 3 goals in a match to be played in Bangkok to take second place in Group C and push China down the table, thus ending their World Cup dreams. All seemed lost for China as the Thai football team was much stronger than Singapore and was expected to achieve their desired result.

But sometimes, in life as well as in football, a hero comes along. Singapore's veteran 40-year-old goalkeeper Hassan Sunny was to become a hero, but more in China than his own country. In the match that ensued, Hassan Sunny played the game of his life, denying the Thai attackers who constantly invaded his goal. Sunny made an astonishing 11 saves in the match, which Thailand won 3–1. No prizes for guessing who the man of the match was. So, thanks to Hassan Sunny's heroics, China nudged Thailand and squeezed into the next round along with group leaders South Korea. But that's not the end of this story.

The beautiful game always finds a way to give back something to its ardent devotees, and that's what makes it so beautiful. Hassan Sunny became an overnight sensation on Chinese social media as he was instrumental in China reaching the Last 18 Asian teams to attempt qualification for the World Cup. Chinese football fans soon got to know that Hassan Sunny had followed his other family members by venturing into the restaurant trade. It was his other passion, and he had a food stall in Singapore. The Chinese fans decided that it was payback time and started visiting Hassan Sunny's food stall as a gesture of their appreciation and love. Now, apart from the sizeable Chinese population that resides in Singapore for work, many tourists also visit the island nation. Football is big in China, and all these Chinese fans started flooding Hassan Sunny's food stall to buy out all his food. Some even started sending him money online, using the stall's QR payment code when they found that they couldn't visit his shop because of other commitments.

Hassan Sunny's food stall serves a variety of local Singaporean dishes, ranging from delicious options like Hainanese chicken rice, laksa (a spicy noodle soup), satay (grilled skewered meat), and mouthwatering rendang. The

Chinese fans who visited the shop discovered that the food served by the man was as good as the man. So, they kept going back for more!

From an overnight football sensation, Hassan Sunny turned into one of the richest food stall owners. Hassan thanked the Chinese fans on social media but also urged them to stop sending him money immediately. This gesture only won him more fans as the Chinese admired his down-to-earth nature as a small shop owner. Hassan Sunny, despite playing for Singapore, has unofficially become the 12th man for the Chinese football team.

Keeping Goal in the Fog

A football match in 1937 was enveloped by a dense fog that made visibility an impossibility. It was Christmas Day as Charlton Athletic and Chelsea faced each other at the Stamford Bridge Stadium in London, England. Suddenly, a heavy fog cast its spell across the pitch, and this fog was so dense that the match was called off. However, as the players and referee sauntered off the pitch, one man was unaware that the match had been abandoned. This was Charlton Athletic's goalkeeper, Sam Bartram, who was still guarding his goalpost, waiting for an attack by Chelsea's strikers. He was happy as Charlton had been dominating Chelsea, and he was secure in the knowledge that his boys had pinned Chelsea to their own half. No one had the courtesy to inform Bartram that the match had been called off. Incredibly, Bartram stood at his post and peered through the fog for as long as 15 minutes, stamping his feet for some warmth before realization finally struck him. Thankfully, a police officer discovered the lone ranger on the field, informed him about what had occurred and escorted him off the pitch. When Bartram reached the warmth of the dressing room, he was greeted with convulsive laughter by the rest of the Charlton team members. If the London police rescued Bartram from the foggy pitch, how could the Press be far behind? The Associated Press published this snippet on 27 December 1937 about the foggy football match:

London (AP) – Goalkeeper Bartram believes a good defence is the backbone of a good football team. When the worst Christmas fog since 1904 settled over the playing field the officials decided to call the game off, but Bartram stuck doggedly to his post, eyes cagily guarding his goal. As soon as play was terminated all the players except Bartram left the field. A searching party finally found him and convinced him it was safe to leave his post.

Scoring All the Goals for Both Teams

When you score 4 goals in a football match, you'd naturally think your teammates would carry you off on their shoulders. Sadly, this wasn't to be the case for Chris Nicholl, who broke a record in 1976 by netting 4 goals in a single game. This happened when Leicester City faced Aston Villa at Filbert Street in March 1976. Aston Villa central defender Chris Nicholl was the cynosure of all eyes when he achieved this feat. However, his heroics were nullified as 2 of the 4 goals were own goals as the Division One match concluded in a 2–2 draw. Nicholl would have been comforted by the fact that he scored 2 goals after those embarrassing own goals as redemption of sorts. He would have wished that he scored a third to seal the win, but then again, it could have also gotten much worse. But those 2 own goals significantly upped Nicholl's tally as he ended up as Leicester's fifth top goal scorer that season despite being a central defender.

The Panenka Penalty

The Panenka penalty was born in Euro 1976 and has been practised and mastered by many footballers since then. If penalty shoot-outs are stressful for players and fans, shoot-outs to decide the final of a major tournament are nerve-racking. So, Antonin Panenka decided to invent a new style of penalty-taking to relieve himself of all the stress that accumulates in a penalty shoot-out. Thanks to his penalty, Czechoslovakia won the 1976 European Championships, the fifth edition of the Euro in a penalty shoot-out after the final with West Germany ended in a 2–2 draw. In the penalty shoot-out that followed, both teams scored their first 3 penalties. Czechoslovakia scored the 4th penalty, and West Germany missed. With the score 4–3 in favour of Czechoslovakia, midfield maestro Antonin Panenka stepped up to take the crucial penalty that would win the match for his country. With so much pressure on a crucial penalty, the player taking it is normally expected to blast the ball in either corner of goal as that maximizes the chances of penalty conversion. This is what most modern players would have done, and this was 1976 after all. But Panenka was as cool as a cucumber and decided to chip the ball straight down the middle, well knowing that the goalkeeper would dive either left or right. This was the most outrageous converted penalty of the game to date in the history of football. Czechoslovakia won the match 5–3 on penalties and were crowned European champions. This style of penalty is known as the Panenka penalty in honour of the man who invented it. Many footballers have tried to recreate the Panenka penalty since then, and Andrea Pirlo came the closest to recreating the original magic at Euro 2012. But no one has done it yet like the great Antonin Panenka!

The Maradona Shrine in God's Own Country

Diego Maradona is revered as a god in Argentina for his heroics on the football field, which won numerous accolades for Argentina, including the 1986 FIFA World Cup. Maradona also has godlike status in the Italian town of Napoli for transforming the club from an ordinary one to a title-winning one. But Maradona also has die-hard fans all across the world in every nook and corner where football is a passion. The southern Indian state of Kerala, also known as God's own country, is no exception. It is also fitting that there exists a Maradona shrine in Kerala. This is basically a hotel room where Maradona had once stayed, which has been converted into a museum cum hotel room now for eight years. But not everyone can stay in this hotel room. Conditions apply. You are only eligible if you are a fan of the legendary Diego Maradona.

The name of the hotel is Blue Nile, and it is located in the Kannur District of Kerala. One day, the owner, V. Ravindran, received a visit from a team representing

Diego Maradona, who had come to inspect hotels for the legend to stay three months before Maradona arrived in India. They selected the Blue Nile and briefed Ravindran about what preparations they wanted to make their celebrity guest at home, without mentioning Maradona's name. Two rooms were joined together to create a large suite room, thus giving birth to Room No. 309. When Ravindran was finally informed that the celebrity guest was none other than Maradona, he was over the moon as he was a huge fan of the footballer. No stone was left unturned to make Maradona feel at home after that. It was like God coming to his own country. Apart from following all the instructions in the list, Ravindran also went out of the way for Maradona. He had read somewhere that Maradona loved Russian cuisine. So, he immediately appointed a chef who had worked in Russia before. A special menu was prepared for Maradona after his arrival, and he mainly ordered prawns, salads, carrots, and sweet lemon juices. Maradona couldn't speak English, so his secretary spoke to Ravindran and his team, serving as his interpreter. Maradona stayed in the Blue Nile for two days, and thousands of people gathered outside the hotel to catch a glimpse of their footballing icon. Scared that the huge crowd might storm the hotel, Ravindran requested Maradona to step out onto the balcony and wave at the crowd. Maradona obliged and was greeted by a thunderous applause, which would have pleased even the gods in heaven. That was a special day for Kannur on 23 October 2012. Maradona was so happy that he hugged Ravindran when saying goodbye after he checked out of the Blue Nile.

When Ravindran received news of Maradona's death years later, he was deeply saddened. He decided to pay tribute to the Argentine legend in his own special way. Room No. 309 was converted into a small museum in honour of Maradona's visit. The accessories used by the legend in the plates, spoons, forks, bed sheets, toiletries, and also the shells of the prawns he had eaten were enclosed and kept in glass frames for visitors to see. Room No. 309 also boasts of rare pictures of Diego Maradona and newspaper clippings about him. The room is rented out to customers as the 'Maradona Special Suite', and two to three guests come to stay at the room every month. Even the great Don Diego would be nodding his approval from the heavens above!

Sheikh It Baby

The 1982 FIFA World Cup was a special one for many reasons. But there was one baffling moment that stood out amidst all the other memorable incidents. This took place during a group game between France and Kuwait. In 1982, France was a great side, and it was baffling in a way that this great French side had never won a World Cup. They did win the Euro in 1984, though. But coming back to the match against Kuwait, the French team completely dominated the field of play. Le Blues were ahead by 4 goals to 1 when something strange happened just after the 4th French goal was scored by Alain Giresse. Sheikh Fahad Al-Ahmad Al-Sabah, the president of the Kuwait Football Association, wanted the 4th French goal disallowed because he claimed that his team had stopped because they had heard another whistle, which they had thought was the referee's whistle. The sheikh threatened that Kuwait would abandon the match unless the goal was disallowed. Much to everyone's surprise, the goal was eventually disallowed in a bizarre decision after the equally bizarre protest. It was the turn of the French team to protest now, but the decision stood. In what could be termed as poetic footballing justice, Maxime Bossis scored again, and the match ended 4–1 in favour of France.

The Conning of Southampton

1996 saw Graeme Souness and Southampton FC make one of the most ridiculous, bizarre and worst signings in the history of football when they took the Senegalese international player Ali Dia in their ranks. The build-up to this signing is reminiscent of a schoolboy prank, and we wonder how Souness and Southampton fell for it. It was a joke, but the Southampton fans were not laughing. It all began when Southampton received a phone call from someone who pretended to be George Weah, a famous football star in several European clubs who went on to become president of Liberia. George Weah recommended Ali Dia highly to Southampton and insisted that they would be getting quite a bargain for the deal. The Southampton officials did not even bother to check if the call had actually come from George Weah and did not even check the credentials of Ali Dia. Instead, they just signed him blindly. When Ali Dia played in the Premier League, he was easily the worst-ever foreign player recruited by the club. All the other clubs had quite a laugh at Southampton's expense.

A Sing and a Miss

The 1992 FIFA World Cup was hosted by the USA for the first time. Football, known as soccer in the USA, had not taken off in a big way then. So, it was great to see the crowds filling the stadiums at USA 92 which holds the record for attendance to date in World Cups. But it all went horribly wrong on the opening day. Someone had decided that American singer Diana Ross would open the month-long tournament with her singing. This was a great idea as Diana Ross is an amazing singer. However, footballers don't sing professionally and singers don't play ball for a living and never the twain shall meet. It wasn't such a great idea for Diana to take a penalty kick. The event was planned such that Diana Ross would kick a football, which would break the goal in half, and she would run onto the stage to do her number. But the folks who planned this completely missed the fact that one should know how to kick a football even if they are kicking it into an open net. So, Diana Ross got ready to kick the football into the open goal, which would activate the stuff that would destroy the goalpost as a stadium full of people watched. Drat! Diana Ross missed the target completely! We suspect that the ghosts of legendary goalkeepers were at work here who did not wish that goalpost to be destroyed by Diana Ross.

The Cold War

A friendly match in football is meant to be... erm friendly, of course. In 1945, the friendly match at White Hart Lane between English club Arsenal and Russian club Dynamo Moscow was supposed to be just that – a friendly! But it turned out instead to be one of the strangest football matches ever played in the history of football. Thick fog had invaded the pitch, making visibility an impossibility sometimes during the match. The players' request for the match to be abandoned was rejected by the referee, who said that the play must go on. It was a friendly, after all. However, both sides were desperate to win the game and began breaking the rules and employing unfair tactics. What followed was astonishing in the modern context of the game. The Russians made a substitute, but the substituted player never left the field. The referee failed to notice the extra man in the thick fog. Some reports suggested that the Russians had fifteen men on the pitch at one time. But this could be an English exaggeration. The English team retaliated in kind. After a player was red-carded and sent off, he slipped in quietly after some time completely unnoticed. After the English goalkeeper lost consciousness because he ran right into his post because of the fog, a fan reportedly took his place at goal. The match finished with Dynamo Moscow emerging as the winners with a 4–3 margin. For the first time, a friendly match became famous for all the wrong reasons.

The Fake Brazil Team in North Korea

When North Korea qualified for the 2010 FIFA World Cup, they realized they had a problem on their hands when it came to practice matches or international friendlies. Not a single country wanted to play in North Korea because of the country's extreme policies and closed economy. In a bizarre move, North Korea recruited a fourth-division Brazilian football team named Atlético de Sorocaba to play against their national team and billed this team as the Brazilian national team to their fans and supporters. This deception was possible because this Brazilian team had been acquired by South Korean religious leader Sun Myung Moon, who had business interests in North Korea. This match took place in 2009, and the Brazilian team was stunned to see a stadium filled with almost 80,000 spectators who had all turned up to see Brazil play their national team. Sorocaba played this match wearing the famous yellow jersey of the Brazilian team and won the match 2–1. Sorocaba played 4 games in the North Korean capital Pyongyang during 2009–15. They lost the second match 0–1 in 2010.

In 2016, Atlético de Sorocaba quit professional football. The club was forced to leave the state's football federation because of financial problems. Ironically, its training facilities are now being used by its once major opponent, São Bento. Paulo Roberto manages this team, and he was one of the fake Brazilian national team players involved in the 2009 Atlético de Sorocaba match in Pyongyang.

The Double Transfer

In a remarkable and unique double transfer, which is the first in football history, Swiss footballer Alisha Lehmann and her Brazilian boyfriend Douglas Luiz were transferred from the EPL club Aston Villa to Juventus. Alisha would play in the Italian Serie A Femminile. This 'couple transfer' was the culmination of Alisha and her partner Douglas's dreams as they had often been separated because of their footballing commitments in different European cities. So, it was a dream come true for the couple as they would be in the same city now. Lehmann has signed a three-year contract with Juventus, and this took place just a week after her boyfriend Luiz signed a five-year contract with the same club. Juventus Femminile, which finished second with 40 points in 2022–23 Serie A, 8 points behind league winners Roma expect to boost their attacking options with the addition of Lehmann, who is an asset when it comes to both scoring goals and providing assists. Her Brazilian boyfriend will strengthen the midfield of Juventus. But he has a lot of work cut out for him as Juventus was seventh on the Serie A table in the 2022–23 season. But this one's surely a couple goal achieved!

The Funniest Gazza Moments

Paul John Gascoigne or Paul Gascoigne or Gazza as he is popularly known was one of the best attacking midfielders produced by England. Gazza was hugely popular in his playing days, and the adulation for him by English football fans came to be known as 'Gazzamania'. Gascoigne is also remembered for his eccentric ways and pranks, which caused a lot of funny moments. From planting snakes in the bedrooms of teammates to naughty deeds in the toilets of 10 Downing Street, Gazza is a legend with his controversies just like his prowess on the pitch. Let's go down memory lane and relive some of Gazza's funniest moments.

The Famous FA Cup Quote

The FA Cup is a prestigious trophy in English football, and Gazza was understandably animated after winning the semi-final in 1991 with Tottenham Hotspur after beating North London rivals Arsenal 1–0. After the win, Gazza famously told reporter Ray Stubbs, 'I'm now away to get my suit measured!' – a line that has risen above the sport according to Gazzamaniacs.

The Dentist Chair

The England team during Gazza's time had a love-hate relationship with the English tabloids, and it was more hate than love. Before the much-anticipated Euro 96 tournament hosted by England, the English squad decided to get together for some team bonding in Hong Kong. Unfortunately, this team-bonding exercise descended into wild parties and alcoholism. No surprise as Gazza was around. The pictures of their nocturnal adventures reached the English press, and the 'dentist chair' celebrations caused quite a public outrage and backlash thanks to the media. Gazza was the cynosure of all eyes as he was being showered in liquor seated in this infamous 'dentist chair' celebration. Gazza decided to reply to his critics in style when he scored with a stunning volley against Scotland and celebrated in a typically dentist chair-esque manner with Steve McManaman and company squeezing a bottle of water in Gazza's face. England breezed past Scotland 2–0. But Gazza and his team lost in the semi-finals to Germany on penalties as the Germans went on to lift the trophy. Only one English player missed his penalty, and he goes by the name of Gareth Southgate.

Gazza and the Ostrich

'Gazza and the Ostrich' sounds like a children's storybook rather than Paul Gascoigne's strange exploit on the Tottenham Hotspurs training ground. When Gazza arrived for training, late as usual, the coach was just about to give him an earful when he saw someone walking alongside Gazza, carrying a big brown sack. The sack was moving as if something or someone was in it. The bag was opened, and out jumped an ostrich wearing a Spurs shirt. As the jerseyed ostrich ran around the pitch, it was noticed that the jersey had a number 7 with SEDGLEY written on the back. This was hilarious as Gazza's teammate Steve Sedgley was nicknamed 'Long Neck'. As the lads almost fell on the ground laughing, Steve Sedgley was probably the only one not amused.

Hold on To Your Hat, John

Soon after signing for Tottenham, Gazza arrived for training with a huge motor home he had recently purchased for his dad. In characteristic Gazza style, he asked one of the caretakers to fix an issue with the roof that needed immediate attention. The unsuspecting caretaker named John Coberman climbed to fix the apparent rattle from the roof. To his great surprise, Gazza simply started the engine and drove off while John hung to the roof for dear life. Gazza drove a long way, and when he returned, poor John was as white as a ghost. Whoever said that the English are boring has to meet Gazza!

Walks Like an Egyptian: The Gazza Strip

As usual, the best one is saved for the last. When Gazza decided to go Egyptian. This was during Italia 90 when England were preparing for their group game against Egypt. The eccentric Gazza decided to entertain his teammates by dressing up as a mummy. He made an appearance at the resort's swimming pool totally wrapped in toilet roll. Now, keep in mind that other guests of the hotel who had no idea about Gazza's eccentric ways were also present by the poolside. But Gazza didn't give a f*ck and dived into the hotel pool in his cheap mummified avatar. Soon, all that toilet roll floated to the surface as Gazza coolly swam a length. Then, he emerged from the pool butt-naked and walked to his room as the horrified public watched and the English players nearly drowned in laughter. This was probably Gazza's best midfield move ever. Thank God he didn't represent England in water polo!

Chelsea's Blues

In April 1997, Chelsea played Coventry City in one of the most bizarre matches of the English Premier League. That's because when Chelsea played away from home at Highfield Road, they realized they didn't have a jersey to play with. In the 1990s, teams in the EPL had only two kits, one for home matches and one for away matches, and there was no concept of a third kit. Chelsea's home strip was light blue, which was the same as Coventry's kit. Coventry was nicknamed the 'Sky Blues' and played all their matches at home in their traditional light blue kit. For some strange reason, Chelsea arrived at Highfield Road without their away kit. The referee logically concluded that the two home kits clashed and play was delayed for 15 minutes as they tried to solve the issue. The only solution was for Coventry to change their jersey or Chelsea to wear Coventry's red and black away kit for the match to take place. Otherwise, Chelsea would have to forfeit the match to Coventry City. Chelsea's high-profile manager, Dutchman Ruud Gullit tried to exert his influence by trying to persuade Coventry to change their kit. But Coventry absolutely refused, and Gullit was forced to play his players in Coventry's second jersey – a red and black checked shirt with Peugeot as the sponsor. So, Chelsea stars like Gianfranco Zola, Roberto Di Matteo, Mark Hughes, and Frank Leboeuf were forced to put on their opponent's jersey while they played against them. This was a sort of psychological victory for Coventry before the start of the game as the Chelsea players looked rather ridiculous in the worst Coventry jersey ever (as claimed by Coventry themselves) matched with the blue Chelsea shorts. Coventry won the match 3–1, and this victory was crucial as, with the 3 points, they narrowly survived being relegated in the next season. Chelsea finished fifth on the table that season. The Chelsea players were so disgruntled after the match that they took their shirts off at the end of the match and threw them on the floor before they came down the tunnel. Sore losers, eh? No team has forgotten to carry their away jerseys since that disastrous mistake by Chelsea.

Penalties Bizarre

One of the football matches that deserves a special place in the list of bizarre incidents in football is definitely the one between Juventud Alianza and General Paz Juniors in the Argentinean football league. The match was in the qualifying round of the Apertura for the Ronda final at the end of the 2009–10 season and was played after General Paz Juniors had won the first leg 2–1. They travelled to Juventud Alianza for the second leg, and this match finished with a 2–1 win by the home team. Now, the aggregate scores were levelled at 3 goals apiece. It was decided that a penalty shoot-out would determine the eventual winner. Thus began the longest penalty shoot-out in football history. As many as 40 penalties were taken without a single one being missed. The scores were still tied at 20–20. Then, the first miss happened to break the prolonged suspense when General Paz Juniors goalkeeper Marcos De Tobillas saved Ruiz's penalty kick. But that also meant that the goalkeeper Tobillas would have to take the next penalty kick, which was penalty number 42. With a cool head, Tobillas struck the ball past his rival goalkeeper, Gonzalez, to earn a victory for his team. This was an amazing match not only for the massive duration but also for the fact that it took a goalkeeper to save a penalty and score the next one himself to ensure a victory for his team.

Coming Back To Life

This bizarre football story took place in February 1993 when English teams Congleton Town and Rossendale faced each other. Before the match got underway in Congleton Town, the management of the team received news of the death of 85-year-old supporter and fan Fred Cope who had supported the club for a long time. Desirous to pay a heartfelt tribute to this old-timer, a few words were hastily written into the match-day programme as the game could not be delayed. A minute's silence was organized before kick-off to pay tribute to him. But what was extremely funny was when the players had formed a ring to observe silence in the middle of the pitch, in walked Mr Cope to take his usual position to watch the match and support the home team. The club officials realized the deadly mistake and used presence of mind to change the minute's silence by paying tribute to former England captain Bobby Moore, who had passed away a few days ago. Mr Cope was terribly surprised to read his own obituary, though, but he returned home a happy man having won the half-time draw. The prize money was £10 and a bonus prize of a whisky bottle.

The Referee's False Teeth

A funny incident during a football game in Denmark saw a goal being disallowed because the referee was busy doing something else and didn't spot the ball going into the goal. In a high-voltage football match between Ebeltoft and Nørager in 1960, Nørager were leading 4–3. In the last seconds of the match, referee Henning Erikstrup tried blowing his whistle to bring the match to a conclusion. But instead, his false teeth flew out to hit the ground. In a desperate attempt to recover his false teeth and save them from being trampled by a footballer's boots, the referee did not end the game. As he was looking for his false teeth, Ebeltoft scored the equalizer to tie the match

4–4. But Erikstrup disallowed the goal, stating that the 90 minutes were up even though he had not blown the whistle. Amidst furious protests by the Ebeltoft players, Nørager were declared the winners. Moral of the story is never hire a referee with false teeth to officiate a football match.

The Curious Case of John Terry

Never believe everything you come to know from social media. That's what football fans were thinking when Chelsea legend John Terry cleared the mystery about a picture that had been circulated on social media for a very long time. The picture showed John Terry celebrating a goal scored against West Ham in front of the opposition supporters as they made obscene gestures towards the former England international. This picture in question claimed that the men making obscene gestures towards John Terry were his own father and uncle, who were die-hard West Ham supporters. The picture became hugely popular on the internet as fans were led to believe that the West Ham gentlemen in it were actually Terry's family members. Many years later, when John Terry was questioned about the picture, he dismissed these claims as absolute rubbish. He found it incredulous, saying that even though his entire family were die-hard West Ham fans, they loved him too much to abuse him. Well, that settled it all right, and hopefully, people won't spread such strange rumours just to get more followers on social media. For the uninitiated, John Terry was once a part of West Ham's youth system before the centre-back decided to sign a professional deal with Chelsea. This earned the

John Terry

displeasure of his father, who was a Hammers supporter and wanted John to play for West Ham. But as a father, he must be proud of John Terry's achievements for both club and country. Aren't we all?

The Strange Norwegian Council

The region in the northern part of Europe is known as Scandinavia and comprises Norway, Sweden, and Denmark. The weather in Scandinavia is extreme, with temperatures going as high as 20–25°C (68–77°F) during the summer months and dropping as low as –20°C (–4°F). Playing football in such extreme temperatures is always challenging, and yet, these countries manage to produce excellent football teams. However, life is not always smooth sailing for footballers like a club side in Norway discovered. Norwegian club side Ny-Krohnborg IL returned to preseason after their winter break and were greeted by a rather strange sight. They found themselves staring at a road covering part of their football field. While the local club were enjoying their hiatus, the city council went ahead with their plan to build a supply road to the new Krohn Minde psychiatric hospital of all things. This was on the campus of Helse Bergen University, which was located right next to Krohnborg's home pitch. The members of the council were obviously no football lovers.

Messi Tales

Lionel Messi has been hailed by many great footballers as the greatest of all time. However, Messi does not score many goals using his head because of his short height. Messi's youth coach tried his best to make Messi take headers at the goal but failed. So, he decided to use an alternative strategy – bribing Messi. The coach discovered that Messi had a weakness for alfajores, which was a mouth-watering confection created out of cookies sandwiching dulce de leche, occasionally covered in chocolate. Initially, the coach rewarded the young Messi with the treat every time he scored a goal. But soon, Messi was eating too many of the alfajores simply because he was scoring too many goals, and this was not a desirable diet for an athlete of any age.

So the coach switched the deal so Messi would only get a treat when he scored a goal with his head. But now, he would get two instead of one. The coach was confident that Messi would not score with a header, but what happened next was incredible. In the next game, Messi dribbled past everyone, including the goalkeeper, to reach the edge of the goalpost. He chipped the ball up and headed it in. Then, he stared at the coach and held up two fingers to seal the treat. That is when the coach realized that bribes wouldn't work with a talent like Messi.

When Lionel Messi arrived at the La Masia youth academy in Barcelona, the older boys were asked to go easy on the new boy because he was really small. In comparison, the rest of the boys like Piqué were a rough bunch. Piqué, in particular, was warned. But all the worries seemed unjustified as Messi was so fast on the pitch that none of the other boys could catch him to inflict any damage.

Messi was simply unstoppable in the 2018 Copa del Ray final for Barcelona against Sevilla. As a last resort, Sevilla defender Sergio Escudero fouled Messi by trying to pull down his shorts as Messi sprinted towards goal. Escudero got a yellow card from the referee because the incident happened near the halfway line. If Messi was closer to goal, Escudero would have surely seen a red card.

A year later, the same incident occurred but with more hilarity. In 2019, during an El Clásico moment between arch-rivals Barcelona and Real Madrid, Toni Kroos pulled down Messi's shorts to stop him, thereby exposing his bum and causing a few laughs in the stadium. This was the only thing that made news about that El Clásico, however, apart from the violent pro-Catalan demonstrations outside the Nou Camp stadium where protestors fought the baton-wielding police. But somehow, the media was more interested in stories about Messi's exposed bum. This was understandable as this was the first goalless clash between Barcelona and Real Madrid in 17 years.

Watching Messi on the pitch immediately after kick-off is a bizarre sight. He simply goes on a stroll around the defence of the opposition, reluctant to touch the ball as he ignores it completely. The first few minutes see Messi saunter about lazily. But, in reality, he looks at each opponent to analyse and study their positions and how the opposition defence is working as a cohesive unit. After storing these visuals in his memory like a supercomputer, Messi goes about his plans to breach the opposition defence, and that's when he touches the ball. As his old coach Pep Guardiola explains, 'After five, ten minutes, he has the map in his eyes and in his brain, to know exactly where is the space and what is the panorama.'

Girlfriend over Country

In a strange incident more reminiscent of old comedy movies, former Irish footballer Stephen Ireland killed his own grandmother. Not literally, of course; he just lied that she was dead. But the reason for this deception is even more bizarre than the lie itself. Ireland did so to avoid national footballing duties and visit his girlfriend in Cork instead because she was feeling lonely. What made things worse for Ireland (both the player and the country) is that the Republic of Ireland lost the match against the

Czech Republic in 2007, which Stephen Ireland chose to avoid. Ireland also asked his Manchester City manager Sven-Göran Eriksson to leave him out of a club fixture because he was still grieving after his grandma's death and needed to help with the funeral arrangements. When it was discovered that Ireland's maternal grandmother, Patricia Tallon, was alive and kicking (not a football, of course), an embarrassed Ireland had to apologize to both club and country. When Eriksson was asked to sum up Ireland's behaviour, he did so in one word – STUPID!

The Crazy Football Manager Stories

The record for the shortest stint as football manager is held by **Leroy Rosenior** who held a manager's position for, hold your breath, just 10 minutes. Rosenior was reappointed as manager of Torquay United just as the club was relegated from the English Football League. But the club was sold just minutes after being relegated, and the new owners wanted their own manager at the helm of affairs. So, poor Leroy Rosenior was sacked.

In a strange move, player–manager **Ivor Broadis** sold himself to another football club in 1949 to improve the finances of the club that he was leaving. In 1946, Broadis was 23 years old when he became the youngest player–manager as he joined Carlisle United. But with the club's finances going on a downward spiral, Broadis sold himself to Sunderland for £18,000 as a player when an opportunity presented itself to improve the financial condition of Carlisle United. This sacrifice paid dividends for Broadis, who was rewarded with 18 caps for England

and a career at Manchester City later. After his playing days, Ivor Broadis returned to his first love, Carlisle, as a journalist for a local newspaper.

French manager **Raymond Domenech** was a strange bird for sure. If it wasn't mad enough to propose to his girlfriend on the pitch right after France were knocked out of Euro 2008, his reign saw a mutiny by the French players at the World Cup just two years later. But everything pales in comparison to what Domenech did when he first took charge of France in 2004. He ended the international career of Robert Pires because he didn't trust Scorpios. This obsession with astrology was dangerous as Domenech did not want Leos on the French team either. His failure at the 2010 World Cup was, hence, written in the stars as was his subsequent dismissal.

There are other football managers who allowed superstition to rule them as well. Among them is the architect of Argentina's triumph at the 1986 World Cup – manager Carlos Bilardo. Once, the Argentine manager asked officials to track down a certain woman who had wished him good luck before the match, which had eventually resulted in a 4–1 victory. After that, Bilardo called the lady before every game, and she wished him good luck. In Mexico 86 as well, Bilardo was at his eccentric and superstitious best, although not causing serious harm to the team. He banned Maradona and company from eating chicken and made the team take taxis to the stadium after Argentina had won a match and their bus had broken down. When you have Diego Maradona in your team, do you really need the stars to be aligned on your side?

Franklin Charles Buckley or Major Buckley epitomized manager eccentricity during the pre-war days. A few would argue that he was majorly ahead of his time, while most would agree that he was simply bonkers. Major Buckley spent 17 long years as manager of Wolverhampton Wanderers when he had ample time to employ his crazy methods, which included having the local fire brigade water the pitch to suit the needs of his team, encouraging his team to go ballroom dancing to improve their balance, and most bizarrely, to inject his players with monkey gland with the hope that it would make them taller to head the ball home. This major had surely gone bananas!

Felix Magath, Fulham manager, was nicknamed 'Saddam' for his dictatorial and gruelling preseason fitness regimes. He also introduced a new policy where he would approve all medical procedures. Defender Brede Hangeland was stunned when he got a dead leg once and was asked to rub cream cheese on the affected area by Magath. Magath's crazy methods also included summoning a player to his office and staring at him for up to five minutes without saying a single word. No wonder he was also called 'the last dictator in Europe'.

When manager **Nathan Jones** took charge of Luton Town in 2016, he desperately wanted to instil a winning culture in a League Two Club that were serious underachievers. He concluded that the squad's obsession with table tennis was detrimental to their performance on the football pitch. So, in a moment of madness, Jones burnt down the table tennis table. But he had to smash up the table first to make it inflammable. This is a classic case of good intention but poor execution. The Hatters boss was certainly mad as a hatter, but his methods led to success for Luton Town the following season. RIP ping pong!

In 1979, Nottingham Forest had won the European Cup and manager Brian Clough was at the height of his powers. His word was the last one at the club and obeyed by everyone. Well, almost everyone. A young 16-year-old apprentice was cleaning the Nottingham Forest dressing room one afternoon when he received a call on the phone there. The familiar voice ordered, 'Young man I want a pot of tea and six cups brought to the boardroom, now.'

The man said he was busy and disconnected. Clough rang again.

'I don't think you understand,' he said and repeated his order.

'Sorry. I don't think you understand. I'm busy,' the apprentice replied and put down the phone again to return to his cleaning.

A furious Clough rang again and asked, 'Do you know who this is on the phone?'

'Yes,' the young player replied, 'the manager, Mr Clough. 'Do you know who I am?' he asked.

'No,' Clough confessed.

'Well make your own f*cking tea then,' the young player replied. He put the phone down and ran out of the dressing room.

Cruyff versus Romario

The two legends Johan Cruyff and Romario did not get along famously as coach and player in Barcelona, which led to Romario quitting unexpectedly in 1995 after a rift with Cruyff. But Brazilian legend Romario was an exceptional player whom any coach would love to have on his team. The only problem was Romario's love for the nightlife and nocturnal adventures that came along with his insane football skills. Mind you, Romario was not into alcohol and was strictly a Coca-Cola guy. But he loved partying and before a 7.30 p.m. kick-off, he would party till 4 a.m., sleep all day and miss practice. Romario's coaches let him do as he pleased as he was so good. Carlos Alberto Parreira excused Romario from the final training camp before the 1994 World Cup because Romario wanted to play beach volleyball with his friends instead. A coach like Johan Cruyff would never permit such a thing. Once, Romario asked Cruyff if he could miss two days of training to make a trip to Brazil to attend the famous carnival in Rio de Janeiro. Cruyff promised to give Romario two days off if he scored 2 goals in the match against Real Madrid the next day. The El Clásico was a big affair, but Romario accepted the challenge. Cruyff's jaw dropped when Romario scored his second goal when the match had just crossed 20 minutes. Then, he gestured to his coach asking to be substituted and permission to leave. Romario told Cruyff that his plane left in an hour, and Cruyff had no choice but to let him go as a promise is a promise after all.

The 100-Hour War after a Football Match

Probably the most infamous and bizarre incident in football was when El Salvador and Honduras went to war presumably over a football match. However, the truth and the roots of this war are more complicated. In 1969, not-so-friendly neighbours El Salvador and Honduras played each other thrice in the qualifying stages of the 1970 FIFA World Cup. The 2 matches that took place in Tegucigalpa on 8 June and San Salvador on 15 June were marred by violence. Stones thrown by Honduran fans at the hotel windows of the El Salvador football team triggered the violence as the Honduran fans intended to disturb the sleep of the El Salvador players before the crucial match. El Salvador lost this match 1–0, and a woman fan named Amelia Bolaños shot herself in despair. When the Honduras team travelled to play in San Salvador, some Honduran fans were killed as an act of revenge for the death of Amelia Bolaños. On the day of the third match, the Salvadoran government cut diplomatic ties with Honduras, and two weeks later, the two countries declared war on each other, complete with aerial bombardment and ground invasion. This is known as the 100-hour war that left 6,000 dead, 15,000 injured and rendered thousands homeless. Thankfully, the war ended four days later after a ceasefire was declared. However, these two countries did not go to war just because of football, and there is a broader context to this conflict. The football matches were just a catalyst for the escalation of the conflict. Despite being a fraction of the size of Honduras, El Salvador boasts of a much larger population. At the beginning of the 20th century, Salvadoran farmers migrated to Honduras in large numbers, mainly because of the availability of land. The 1960s saw the escalation of tension in Honduras over land ownership by the large population of Salvadoran immigrant farmers. The violence against the Salvadorans in Honduras made the San Salvador government accuse Honduras of genocide. The football matches only escalated a deeper existing conflict to result in a full-fledged war.

Man of the Match Awards out of Africa

The Man of the Match or the Player of the Match in football is a prestigious award where the best player of the game is rewarded with this prize. Now, the rewards may vary globally, but nowhere are these awards as interesting, funny and bizarre as the continent of Africa. From live chickens to mobile data to whatnot, here are the goodies gifted to the best players of a match by some African football leagues.

- Mamelodi Sundowns captain Hlompho Kekana broke the internet in 2018 for receiving 5GB of mobile data as his Man of the Match award. Telecom giant Telkom sponsored this award since 2014, and this prize was treasured in African regions where high-speed internet was often a premium. Hope they have increased the quantity of mobile data since then.
- In 2017, the Zimbabwean Premier League started awarding a crate of beer as their Player of the Match prize with Castle Lager as a sponsor. Hope they graduate to champagne someday, which is a norm with the richer leagues.
- Midfielder George Maluleka of the Kaizer Chiefs of South Africa received an oversized credit card in 2014 from Absa Bank as his Man of the Match award. We

just hope George is not too much in debt already.

- In 2019, Nyasa Big Bullets striker Hassan Kajoke received a live chicken from local fans after his Man of the Match performance. The chicken was handed over to the bewildered striker in painted red stripes, reflective of the team colours. Hassan must have been really hungry after that match.
- Finally, the top Man of the Match award from Africa, easily displacing all the other weird and strange gifts. In 2015, a Ghanaian Division One League Man of the Match winner made the headlines for his award. Dreams FC player Emmanuel Sowah Adjei was given a pair of slippers as a prize. Whoever complains about not having adequate budgets in football should definitely be reading this. Slippers for Emmanuel Sowah Adjei to walk on the wild side!

Free Drinks for the First Scorer

Zimbabwe was not the only country to offer beer as a prize to its footballers. An Austrian brewery offered to supply a lifetime's supply of free beer to the first Austrian who would score in the Euro 2008 tournament. It looks like it wasn't incentive enough for the Austrian football team as they managed to score just 1 goal in Euro 2008, and even that was a penalty. Ivica Vastić scored the penalty and has been guzzling free beer ever since.

Amused to Death

Sometimes, your sense of humour can be killing. That is what Lazio midfielder Luciano Re Cecconi discovered in 1978 when he walked into a jewellery shop in Rome. Deciding to play a prank on the owner, he shouted in Italian, 'Stop! This is a robbery!'

Sadly, the shop owner was a man without humour but with a loaded gun. He shot Luciano, who died trying to explain that it was a practical joke. Don't try this in Rome!

How To Stop Football Hooligans... the Romanian Way

Pitch invasions by football hooligans are nothing new in football and quite a nuisance when they happen as they disrupt play and may cause serious accidents. Lots of methods are used in modern football to stop these invasions, like police deployment and electric fences. When it comes to serious pitch invasions and clashes between supporters, the Romanian fourth division is one of the least desirable places in world football. In 2003, the club Steaua Nicolae Balcescu was threatened with expulsion from the league because of the continuous pitch invasions and skirmishes by their supporters. Alexandra Cringus, chairman of the club, decided that the best way to stop these hooligans was to build a moat around the football pitch that would be infested with crocodiles. Why he came up with such a weird idea is anyone's guess, but this shows a lack of vision by the management and displays exactly why Steaua Nicolae Balcescu were still stuck in the fourth division of Romanian football. Cringus did not cringe at this foolhardy plan and proposed that the crocodiles be fed on meat from the local abattoir after they had been acquired. Thank God he didn't suggest feeding the crocodiles with hooligan meat. He also suggested that the ditch be built wide enough so that no one could jump over it and would have to play with the crocs if they were silly enough to make such an attempt. He was confident that this plan would end hooligans running onto the pitch once and for all. But this wasn't some random plan as Cringus had put in considerable thought about health and safety standards as well. The moat would be built far from the pitch so that the players and officials wouldn't fall to their doom. The manager had also thought about those poor crocodiles, you know. As Romanian winters were particularly harsh, he had planned that the water in the moat would be heated by electric pipes to keep the crocs warm and happy. But Cringus had not given any thought to what the local authorities would have to say about his dangerous scheme, which they immediately rejected. No surprises there!

Dogs in Football

A dog is the only animal that saved an English team from being relegated. In 1987, it was the last day of the season, and Torquay United were playing a match that would decide their fate in the English league. In the final few minutes of the match with Crewe Alexandra, Torquay was trailing 2–1. That is when a dog named Bryn came to Torquay's rescue. The police dog was patrolling the touchline with his handler, and rather uncharacteristically, bit the thigh of a Torquay player. The referee stopped the clock, and it took 4 minutes to treat the wound caused by Bryn. In the 4th minute of injury time when play resumed, a dramatic equalizer was scored by Torquay striker Paul Dobson, which saved his team from being relegated. After the dog named Bryn died, he was stuffed and put on display in the Torquay boardroom and honoured as the dog that saved the club from relegation. It's true that a dog's bark is worse than his bite!

Police dogs seem to have a history in football. While they are famous for their discipline and self-control, something about football seems to make them go berserk, just like their best friends. In Brazil, there was an intense game in progress between Náutico and Retrô. In the second half, a police dog invaded the pitch and stole the show. The seriousness of the game disappeared when the dog grabbed hold of the football. This was the Brazilian football state championship final, the Campeonato Pernambucano 2022, and this German Shepherd decided to join in and show off its solo skills with the ball. The players were sporting enough to let the Brazilian four-legged star have some fun. Even dogs in Brazil are crazy about football!

A dog invaded a football pitch in Potosi, Bolivia, as well and took possession of a football boot for as long as 3 minutes, which is a far better record than many football teams of today in terms of ball possession. The dog ran around the length of the field with the boot in its mouth before being escorted off the field by a player from the home team.

In the 1978 FIFA World Cup hosted by Argentina, Scotland had a horrid start. At the press conference after the match, coach Ally MacLeod was facing a barrage of criticism from Scottish journalists when a dog strolled into the room. MacLeod sadly remarked that the dog was his only friend in the room. But when he bent down to stroke the dog, it bit him. That's when MacLeod realized he had no friends and that dogs in Argentina looked friendly, but in reality, they were not.

Roberto Baggio's Tryst with Penalties

Roberto Baggio is one of Italy's most celebrated players and is lovingly known as Il Divin Codino or the 'Divine Ponytail'. But sadly, Baggio could never win the World Cup for the Azzurri. Baggio was the star of the 1994 World Cup, scoring 5 goals as Italy marched to the final, where they faced a mighty Brazilian team. The game went into penalty shoot-outs, and Baggio missed the decisive penalty and Italy lost the final. This was an unfortunate moment and the worst in Baggio's career, which would haunt him forever. He was the team's penalty taker after all and had missed when it mattered the most.

Roberto Baggio never shied away from his responsibilities as penalty taker but there was a time when he had refused to take a penalty against a former club. When Roberto Baggio had been transferred from Fiorentina to Juventus in the Italian Serie A, loyal Florence fans had rioted on the streets. Such was Baggio's popularity. The decisive moment came when Juventus played Fiorentina and the Juventus coach Luigi Maifredi asked Baggio to take a penalty against his former club. Baggio refused to step up simply because if he missed the penalty, Juventus supporters would think that he was favouring his former club. The Juve player eventually taking the penalty missed, and this miss turned out to be crucial as Juventus lost the match 1–0. Maifredi was furious with Roberto Baggio and immediately substituted him after the penalty refusal.

Jamie Carragher and the Flying Coin

English footballer of Irish descent Jamie Carragher had an illustrious career for England and Liverpool. Carragher made 38 appearances for England, but the central defender became a legend for Liverpool, making over 500 appearances for the club and winning several titles, including the famous UEFA Champions League triumph in 2005. Jamie Carragher made his debut for Liverpool in 1997 as a 19-year-old and spent 16 years at the club before announcing his football retirement to become a successful football pundit. His funniest or most bizarre moment on the pitch was when he was struck by a £1 coin which was thrown at him from the crowd when Liverpool locked horns with Arsenal in a 2002 FA Cup match. A furious Carragher threw the coin back at the crowd, and this rush of blood to the head not only earned him a red card but also a £40,000 club fine. What was worse was he also lost his place in the England team temporarily. Moral of the story is that you have to keep a cool head on the pitch even if you have Irish blood running in your veins.

Pigs Flying through the Transfer Window

In a bizarre transfer window in Romania in 1998, Romanian midfielder Ionuț Radu was sold by Second Division club Jiul Petroșani to Râmnicu Vâlcea. But what made this transfer fee crazy was that there was no monetary transaction involved. Instead, Radu was sold for 500 kg of pork, the approximate value then being £1,750. In an astonishing move, Jiul Petroșani club president justified the transfer by stating that the meat would be sold to pay outstanding player salaries. Someone calculated just for fun then that if Cristiano Ronaldo made the £100 million transfer from Real Madrid to PSG during that period, as football gossip suggested, and if he had to be paid in terms of pork, it would amount to almost 29 million kilograms of pork. That's around 6,30,000 pigs. Of course, in current form, as the recent Euros have displayed, the once-upon-a-time GOAT CR7 wouldn't fetch so many pigs now for sure.

A Unique and Unmatched Hat-trick

Hat-tricks are common in football, although it takes a special player to achieve a hat-trick, which is basically an individual scoring 3 goals in the same match. But no one has accomplished the feat achieved by Alvin Martin, according to the BBC. This is understandable because West Ham and England defender Alvin Martin scored a unique hat-trick against Newcastle United in April 1986, a match which West Ham won 8–1. Martin scored 3 goals against three different goalkeepers in the match, making this hat-trick enter the record books. The first goal was scored

West Ham 8–1 Newcastle, 1986

against goalkeeper Martin Thomas, who got injured after some time to be replaced by goalkeeper Chris Hedworth. Alvin Martin then put one past the substitute goalkeeper to take his goal tally to 2. Towards the end of the match, Newcastle replaced Hedworth with Peter Beardsley. Alvin Martin promptly netted his third goal by beating the third goalkeeper to score this remarkable hat-trick. Replicating this feat will be tough for sure.

INDEX